A History of Women's
Education in England

OPEN UNIVERSITY PRESS
Gender and Education Series

Editors
ROSEMARY DEEM
*Senior Lecturer in the School of Education at the
Open University*
GABY WEINER
*Principal Lecturer in Education at
South Bank Polytechnic*

The series provides compact and clear accounts of relevant research and practice in the field of gender and education. It is aimed at trainee and practising teachers, and parents and others with an educational interest in ending gender inequality. All age-ranges will be included, and there will be an emphasis on ethnicity as well as gender. Series authors are all established educational practitioners or researchers.

TITLES IN THE SERIES

Boys Don't Cry
Sue Askew and Carol Ross

Science and Technology in the Early Years
Naima Browne (ed.)

Untying the Apron Strings
Naima Browne and Pauline France (eds)

Changing Perspectives on Gender
Helen Burchell and Val Millman (eds)

Co-education Reconsidered
Rosemary Deem (ed.)

Women Teachers
Hilary de Lyon and Frances Widdowson Migniuolo (eds)

Girls and Sexuality
Lesley Holly (ed.)

A History of Women's Education in England
June Purvis

Whatever Happens to Little Women?
Christine Skelton (ed.)

Dolls and Dungarees
Eva Tutchell (ed.)

Just a Bunch of Girls
Gaby Weiner (ed.)

Women and Training
Ann Wickham

A History of Women's Education in England

June Purvis

Open University Press
Milton Keynes · Philadelphia

Open University Press
Celtic Court
22 Ballmoor
Buckingham
MK18 1XW

and
1900 Frost Road, Suite 101
Bristol, PA 19007, USA

First Published 1991

British Library Cataloguing in Publication Data

Purvis, June
  A history of women's education in England – (Gender and
  education series).
  1. England. Women. Education. History
  I. Title II. Series
  376.941

  ISBN 0–335–09775–8

Library of Congress Cataloging-in-Publication Available

Typeset by Colset (Pte.) Limited, Singapore
Printed in Great Britain by St Edmundsbury Press
Bury St Edmunds, Suffolk

For my beloved daughter, Catherine Malvina

Contents

Series Editor's Introduction

June Purvis's volume breaks new ground by being the first in the series to take a historical perspective; her focus is on the many nineteenth century feminist struggles for educational access and equality and the educational experiences of many ordinary women. The book concentrates mostly on 1800 to 1914, a period of time which saw some quite remarkable changes in the education available to girls and women, whilst nevertheless also subjecting many of them to processes of gender differentiation and segregation. Discrimination against women was as much a feature of private provision as of the gradually developing system of elementary education. June Purvis presents a picture in which the significance of class as well as gender and the importance of ideology as well as curriculum and pedagogy is clearly portrayed. The story presented here demonstrates how difficult it was for women to escape from their domestic role, whatever their social position, but at the same time suggests that education was for many a liberating experience. It is not then, a 'dry' historical discussion but contains many extracts from girls and women themselves talking or writing about what their education meant in personal terms. Many of us wrapped up in the present and day-to-day concerns of education could easily forget the importance of understanding how we got here; this book not only offers a readily accessible way of acquiring this knowledge but also points out many of the historical parallels between the nineteenth century and the present time, especially in relation to attempts to centralize control over state education. If we have not always learnt crucial lessons from history in the past, perhaps now it is time for women to do so.

Rosemary Deem

Acknowledgements

This book has grown from research I undertook while at the Open University for a doctoral thesis on the lives and education of working-class girls and women in nineteenth-century England. My research supervisor, Madeleine Arnot, taught me much; she was constantly critical and yet supportive of all that I wrote and I gratefully thank her. This research was subsequently written up in my book *Hard Lessons, The Lives and Education of Working-Class Women in Nineteeneth-Century England* (Oxford, Polity Press, 1989). I would like to thank Polity Press for allowing me to use extracts from my book. Having investigated the lives and education of females within the 'lower' classes of Victorian society, it was but a natural step to research the education available to their more fortunate middle-class sisters.

The publishers of *History of Education*, Taylor and Francis, Ltd., kindly gave me permission to re-use material which first appeared in two articles entitled 'Working-class women and adult education in nineteenth-century Britain', published in 1980 (Vol. 9, No. 3) and ' "Women's life is essentially domestic, public life being confined to men" (Comte): separate spheres and inequality in the education of working-class women, 1854–1900', published in 1981 (Vol. 10, No. 4). Len Barton, Stephen Walker, Ivor Goodson and Stephen Ball granted permission to use material from my articles in their edited collections: 'The double burden of class and gender in the schooling of working-class girls in nineteenth-century England, 1800–1870' in *Schools, Teachers and Teaching* edited by L. Barton and S. Walker (Lewes, Falmer Press, 1981) and 'The experience of schooling for working-class boys and girls in nineteenth-century England' in *Defining the Curriculum: Histories and Ethnographies* edited by I.F. Goodson and S.J. Ball (Lewes, Falmer Press, 1984).

I would like to thank Rosemary Deem for inviting me to write this book, and also for the useful comments and she and Gaby Weiner, as editors of the Gender and Education series with the Open University Press, made on the first draft of this manuscript. Finally, I would like to thank all those women, past and present, who in various ways have helped me to find women's history such a stimulating area of study.

Introduction

This book, written from a socialist feminist perspective, offers an overview of the history of education for girls and women in England from 1800 to 1914. As a socialist feminist I am concerned with analysing the social class divisions between women in nineteenth-century capitalist society, as well as examining the power relationships between the sexes whereby women remained inferior and unequal in comparison with men in their own social grouping. Thus social class and gender differentiation are key themes of this book.

Investigating the class position of girls and women is, however, highly problematic since definitions of social class from the nineteenth century to the present day are mainly based on the occupational differences between men.[1] In particular, women[2] in the past were mainly found in unpaid work, such as housework and childcare, and in forms of waged work that were 'less skilled', lower paid, less unionized and involved less exercise of authority than the jobs of their menfolk. Such dilemmas pose many difficulties for the researcher. One solution, which I adopt here, is to use the conventional terms 'middle-class women' and 'working-class women' while recognizing that such phrases refer to women whose menfolk were classified as middle class and working class, respectively.

In this book, use is also made of a word common in feminist vocabulary – 'patriarchy'. Though patriarchy once referred to the authority of the father, husband or male elder, feminist writers use the term to refer to those processes by which men dominate and exercise control over women. However, this does not mean that patriarchy is always total, fixed or secure nor that women just submit to it. Women do resist male domination and, as the London Feminist History Group points out, the form of women's resistance will differ, depending on whether the women concerned are women of colour or white women, and according to their access to social and economic power.[3] Although I have found hardly any references in the historical sources to women of colour, we shall see in this book that both working-class and middle-class women did struggle against patriarchy as a power structure in the past.

The question is frequently asked – why should we study women's educational past? Isn't it more important to focus on the present? In reply to those questions I would like to make two key points. First of all, histories of education have usually made the female sex 'invisible' and taken boys and men as the main reference groups; thus girls and women have been hidden under such blanket terms as 'children' and 'the people'. Yet, as this book and others reveal, we cannot assume that the educational experiences of the male sex were the same or even similar for girls and women. Secondly, the present is a product of the past and, as Deirdre Beddoe points out, we are moulded and conditioned by a past of which we are alarmingly ignorant.[4] In particular, in the period 1800–1914 we can identify key concerns about educating the female sex that still influence and shape educational experiences.

When I was researching material for this book, it became clear to me that ideas about woman's social position in Victorian society impinged upon and influenced the shape and form of female education. Thus in Chapter 1 I discuss that influential Victorian domestic ideology which upheld that women should ideally be located within the home, as full time wives and mothers. If girls and women were to be educated primarily for the home, then it follows that certain kinds of education would be considered 'more appropriate' than others. In Chapters 2 and 3, respectively, the education of working-class girls and women is discussed. Chapters 4 and 5 focus on the educational experiences of the female sex in the middle classes with only brief reference being made to those in the upper class. Finally, in Chapter 6, a number of themes throughout the book are brought together and their relevance discussed briefly in relation to the education of girls and women to-day.

References

1 Especially influential here was the nineteenth-century economist and philosopher Karl Marx who, in 1848, defined two main classes in

capitalist society, the bourgeoisie and the proletariat, mainly in terms of the male sex. For some present day feminist critiques of this continued emphasis upon men's occupations, lives and experiences for classifications of social class see Stanworth (1984) and Walby (1986).

2 The category 'woman' is not fixed or static but changes in relation to historical and social circumstances. In the nineteenth century, a woman was usually defined as a female aged 14 years old and above – see Walvin (1978), p. 13.

3 London Feminist History Group (1983), p. 1.

4 Beddoe (1983), p. 6.

CHAPTER 1

Woman's Sphere is the Home

Victorian society was clearly stratified by social class. This is encapsulated in some lines from that well-known nineteenth-century hymn, *All Things Bright and Beautiful*:

The rich man at his castle
The poor man at his gate
God made them high and lowly
And ordered their estate.

The different social class experiences of women and men, however, were gendered: as Davidoff and Hall argue, consciousness of class always takes a gendered form, even though the articulation of class and gender is never a perfect fit.[1] In particular, women in all social groupings learnt about the patriarchal nature of Victorian society whereby women, in comparison with men, were second-class citizens.

Legally, for example, before the passing of the Married Women's Property Act in 1882, any income or property a woman possessed would be transferred to her husband on marriage. Thus in 1877, when Millicent Garrett Fawcett (who emerged in the 1880s as one of the leaders of the women's suffrage movement) gave evidence in court regarding the theft of her purse at Waterloo station, she read on the charge sheet that the thief was charged with 'stealing from the person of Millicent Fawcett a purse containing £1.18s. 6d., the property of Henry Fawcett'. Full of indignation, Millicent felt that she had been charged with theft herself, of her own belongings.[2] The subordinate and dependent status of woman within marriage was further reinforced by the legal ruling, not abolished until 1884, that a married woman could be imprisoned for denying her husband 'his' conjugal rights. It is not surprising that in 1851 one angry writer complained that a married woman belonged to and was the property of man, ranked amongst his goods and chattels.[3]

Victorian domestic ideology

The patriarchal nature of Victorian society was evident however not only in the legal inequalities that women experienced, but also in a wide range of social, economic, political and educational practices which subordinated women. Part of the explanation for this state of affairs may be attributed to an influential *domestic ideology* that was firmly established within the dominant middle-class culture by the middle of the nineteenth century. As Davidoff and Hall point out, the period from 1780–1850 was one in which the idea of separate spheres for men and women became sanctified in middle-class thought and practice. Women were identified with the private domain of home and the family as wives and mothers or unmarried dependents; men, on the other hand, were associated with the public sphere of paid work, politics and business and with economic and jural responsibility for their wives and the expected brood of children. Various religious groups, such as the Evangelicals, Unitarians and Quakers, were especially influential in propagating such ideas.[4]

As I have argued elsewhere, middle-class domestic ideology embodied three major assumptions which were frequently emphasised in the writings and sayings of middle-class commentators.[5] First, the notion of separate spheres was advocated as a 'natural' division, based upon the biological differences between men and women. Sarah Lewis, in her widely read *Woman's Mission*, which was first published in 1839 and had gone through 13 editions by 1849, advised that the immense influence which women possess would be most beneficial 'if allowed to flow in its natural channels, viz. – domestic ones'. Greg in 1862 compared women's 'natural duties and labours' as wives and mothers with their 'artificial' task of earning a living.[6]

A second assumption in middle-class domestic ideology was that since women were primarily wives and mothers, they were essentially 'relative' rather than autonomous beings, defined in relation to men and children. The epitome of this view was expressed by that profilic and popular writer on woman's sphere, Sarah Stickney

Ellis who pronounced that women 'are, in fact, from their own constitution, and from the station they occupy in the world, strictly speaking, relative creatures'.[7] The stress upon the *relative* nature of woman's existence was given strong verbal support throughout the nineteenth century. In the late 1860s A Mother advised her readers that a woman's life must be one of self abnegation since man was not made to minister to woman – woman was made for man. Samuel Smiles, a popular writer of 'improving' literature, proclaimed that woman in her various relations of mother, sister, lover and wife was the natural cherisher of infancy, the instructor of childhood, the guide and counsellor of youth, and the confidant and companion of manhood.[8]

Though the relative nature of women was questioned by a number of feminists throughout the Victorian era, it was linked to another assumption within middle-class domestic ideology, namely that women were inferior and subordinate to men. Thus the daughters of England were advised in 1842 that 'the first thing of importance is to be content to be inferior to men' while John Ruskin, the influential writer and art critic, advocated in 1865 that such knowledge should be given to women that would enable them to understand 'and even to aid, the work of men'.[9] Indeed, some practitioners in the medical profession believed that women had a fixed stock of energy which would be rapidly depleted, with disastrous consequences for childbearing, if women's weak brains were taxed with a lot of mental work. Thus Dr Withers Moore, in his presidential address to the British Medical Association in 1886, warned:

> From the eagerness of woman's nature competitive brainwork among gifted girls can hardly but be excessive, especially if the competition be against the superior brain-weight and brain-strength of man. The resulting ruin can be averted – if it be averted at all – only by drawing so largely upon the woman's whole capital stock of vital force and energy as to leave a remainder quite inadequate for maternity.[10]

Ideas about woman's inferiority to man were frequently related also to the belief that women should be subordinate to men and self-sacrificing, especially in the household. Not unexpectedly, Sarah Ellis in 1843 advised the wives of England that self and selfish gratifications should be subservient to a husband's needs, even when he was out of the home, and about to return home.[11] Indeed, as late as 1898, the ninety-fourth revised edition of a popular household advice book offered the following hints for wives:

> If your husband looks a little troubled when he comes home, do not say to him, with an alarmed countenance, 'What ails you, my dear?' Don't bother him; he will tell you of his own accord, if need be. Be observant and quiet. Let him alone until he is inclined to talk; take up your book or your needlework pleasantly and cheerfully; and wait until he is inclined to be sociable. Don't let him ever find a shirt-button missing. A shirt-button being off a collar or wristband has frequently produced the first impatient word in married life.[12]

The influence of middle-class domestic ideology in Victorian society helped to create and maintain gender stereotypes: thus femininity became identified with domesticity, service to others, subordination and weakness while masculinity was associated with life in the competitive world of paid work, strength and domination. Yet, as Davidoff and Hall observe, such gendered characteristics contained many contradictions: for example, idealized femininity was asexual and chaste, yet the supreme goal for women was marriage and motherhood, conditions which publicly proclaimed a woman's sexuality.[13] Nevertheless, the idea of separate spheres for the sexes was pervasive and there is evidence to suggest that certain sections of the working classes themselves, especially from 1870–1914, increasingly supported such a domestic ideology for their own womenfolk. Male trade unionists in the 1870s, for example, often supported the idea that a woman's place was at home. At the Trades' Union Congress, held in Leicester in 1877, Henry Broadhurst proclaimed that union men felt that it was their duty as men and husbands to bring about 'a condition of things where their wives should be in their proper place at home, seeing after their house and family, instead of being dragged into the competition amongst the great and strong men of the world'.[14] Such ideas became an important part of the development of working-class 'respectability'. In particular, the notion that a working-class husband could maintain his family became synonymous with 'manhood'.[15]

Middle-class domestic ideology developed within a particular social, political and economic framework that helped to establish its success in practice. In particular, the development from the late eighteenth century to the mid-nineteenth of an industrial, commercial and factory system outside the home helped to separate workplace and homeplace and thus to create a division between production and consumption, between the public domain of 'work' and the private sphere of 'home'. Although such a division became most pronounced in middle-class households, working-class families were influenced by such changes too.

Most Victorian working-class wives had, of necessity, to engage in paid work in order to supplement the family income. At the beginning of the nineteenth century, many such women were part of a family unit engaged in various 'cottage' industries, such as lacemaking, weaving, glovemaking, strawplaiting. Under such circumstances, a wife and mother could combine her tasks of earning a living, bringing up a family and doing household chores. But by the middle of the nineteenth century, she experienced a marked change in her circumstances since frequently her husband now worked not as part of a home based unit but as a wage earner in the outside world. For many working-class wives and mothers, especially those with small children, the option of paid work outside the home was not feasible. Many had little choice but to remain at home, undertaking poorly paid, home-based sweated work (such as sewing) which might be fitted around domestic tasks and hidden from public view. Although such women were paid workers, they were primarily seen as 'housewives', isolated beings who were separated from other worlds outside the home.[16]

By the middle of the nineteenth century, the 'housewife' had a particular responsibility – creating a secure, harmonious, restful and comfortable 'haven' to which her husband could retreat after his day's work in the harsh, competitive world outside. As Mayhew, an influential journalist and social investigator, proclaimed in 1852:

> the dwelling of the family has ever been considered in this country as a kind of social sanctuary – a spot sacred to peace and goodwill, where love alone is to rule, and harmony to prevail . . . and where the gracious trustfulness and honied consolation of woman, makes ample atonement for the petty suspicions and heartlessness of strangers.[17]

'Ladies' and 'women'

Though the dominant middle-class domestic ideology identified all women with domesticity, different ideals of femininity were espoused for women in different social classes. Thus the ideal of femininity that the middle classes upheld for their own womenfolk was that of the *ladylike homemaker* while the ideal upheld for working-class women was that of the *good woman*. Such class-specific ideals helped to maintain the differences between women and to maintain the status quo rather than to encourage a common union between all women.

These ideals related to a broad distinction that became firmly established within middle-class culture by the 1860s, that between *ladies* and *women*. The class nature of this differentiation is revealed in Mrs Ranyard's description of the work of Bible-women in the homes of the London poor:

> The 'woman' goes where the 'lady' might not enter, and performs offices which are most fittingly rendered by persons of the working class. The floor is scrubbed by a good 'woman' better than by a pious 'lady'. Yet the lady can find the scrubbing brush, and the soap, and materials for soup, and supplies of clothing, and the funds that are needful, and the sympathy and counsel which are indispensable, and be very blessed in her deed.[18]

Such social class differentiation between women pervaded social life. In the 1880s, for example, one could find separate competitions for 'Ladies' and 'Women' at the annual village flower show. While the ladies competed with elegant floral arrangements, the women were not expected to be interested in such things: their competitions were for laundry-work, ironing, preserving, and sewing plain shirts. In addition, the 'women' who won various prizes were referred to by their full names 'with no nonsense about Miss'.[19]

The ideal form of femininity upheld by the middle classes for their own womenfolk, the *ladylike homemaker*, was a being who was expected to be a competent manager of a household but not to engage in routine domestic tasks herself; these were undertaken by servants. As one commentator remarked, a 'rich lady' has many servants, not because there is any pleasure in ordering people about but because she wants 'to save her own time and thoughts by hiring other people to do . . . what she likes to have done'; then her mind 'is free for her children, her friends, her books and all the serious things she has to think of'.[20] For the majority of middle-class women, of course, the ideal of the cultured lady of leisure with an array of servants never materialized since it demanded a level of income that was beyond their financial means.[21] Even so, the employment of a young maid-of-all-work, who did most of the household drudgery, gave at least an air of gentility.

A ladylike wife and mother was not expected, under any circumstances, to engage in paid work – although her 'duties' could include
unpaid philanthropic work amongst the poor. As Margaretta Greg
wrote in her diary in 1853:

> A lady to be such, must be a mere lady, and nothing else. She must
> not work for profit, or engage in any occupation that money can
> command, lest she invade the rights of the working classes, who live
> by their labour.[22]

Octavia Hill who, in 1856, accepted a salary of about £25 a year
for being a secretary to classes for women attending the London
Working Men's College, felt herself to be at a disadvantage with the
voluntary workers since she had 'never before been paid for social
work' and disliked the necessity.[23] Despite the discomfort that
Octavia and many other 'necessitous' middle-class women experienced, the idea that a 'lady' did not 'work' was pervasive. In middle-
class Manchester in the early twentieth century Katherine Chorley
remembered that no woman in her family's circle had a career or
a paid job since it would have cast 'an unbearable reflection of
incompetence upon the money-getting male'.[24]

Being ladylike also involved learning a complex ritual of etiquette. The codes of conduct expected in introductions, cards and
calling, for example, allowed the people involved to decide whether
they wanted to accept or reject social interaction.[25] Similarly, certain unwritten rules governed a lady's behaviour in public places.
Thus Mrs Peel remembers that in London in the 1890s, young ladies
seldom walked out alone nor drove alone in a hansom cab – and
never did a lady travel on the top of an omnibus![26]

As will be apparent from much that has been discussed in this
chapter, extensive, systematic education was not advocated as an
essential aspect of the ideal of the ladylike wife and mother. Indeed,
since women, in comparison with men, were generally believed to
be less original in their thinking, less creative and less capable
of reasoning, their intellectual attainments were not praised.[27]
Intellectual education was supposed to make a woman into that
monstrous being, a 'bluestocking', whose erudition frightened men
and made her physically unattractive.

In contrast to the prescriptive ideal of femininity upheld for
middle-class women, the ideal supported by the middle classes
for women in the 'lower' orders, that of the *good woman*, had a
different emphasis. While the good woman was to be a wife and

mother, located within the home, she was essentially a practical housekeeper, who did her own cooking, childcare and general housework – all in a thrifty, methodical and prudent manner. Thus in 1855 the Rev. James Booth advocated that the daughters of the working classes should be brought up to fit them for their lot in life as the wives and mothers of men in their own station, by being taught a range of practical tasks – such as lighting a fire, sweeping a room, washing dishes, washing clothes, baking bread, dressing a dinner and choosing meat or fish or vegetables. In addition, Booth could not refrain from recommending that working-class women were also taught 'the use of savings banks' and 'the results of thrift', common sentiments expressed in middle-class 'improving' literature for the 'lower' orders of society.[28] Indeed, the maxim 'Heaven helps those who help themselves' was a frequent message directed at working-class women and the working classes generally. Samuel Smiles began his celebrated *Self-Help*, first published in 1859, with these very words.[29]

The ideal of the *good woman* was seen as a solution to many of the problems accompanying industrialization and urbanization, especially the 'problems' of working-class life, e.g. alcoholism, crime, the high infant mortality rate. It was a means of civilizing the working classes and creating, in a diluted form, that mode of family life considered 'respectable', i.e. a wage earning husband and a full time wife and mother. In particular, it was the working-class woman engaged in paid work *outside* the home, especially in the mill or factory, who was seen as a degraded being whose condition needed to be 'raised' for the good of society. Yet again, Smiles had something to say on the matter:

> The factory system, however much it may have added to the wealth of the country, has had a most deleterious effect on the domestic condition of the people. It has invaded the sanctuary of home, and broken up almost all social and family ties. It has torn the wife from the husband, and the children from the parents. Especially has its tendency been to lower the sacred character of woman. The performance of the domestic duties is her proper office in civilized life, – the management of her household, – the rearing and educa-tion of her children, – the economising of the family means, – and the supply of the family wants. But the factory tears her from all these duties: homes become no longer homes; children grow up uneducated and entirely neglected; the domestic affections are crushed or blunted, and woman is no longer the gentle sustainer of man, but his fellow-drudge and fellow-labourer.[30]

Nearly thirty years later, Smiles expounded the same message, pointing out that the moral atmosphere of a home was dependent upon 'good mothers'; when the poorest dwelling was presided over by a 'virtuous, thrifty, cheerful and cleanly woman' then it could become a place 'of comfort, virtue, and happiness'.[31]

By the middle of the nineteenth century then, an influential domestic ideology was established within the dominant middle-class culture. Within this ideology, class-specific ideals of femininity helped to reinforced social class differences between women and also to shape the forms and content of women's education. However, as indicated in the Introduction, girls and women were not passive recipients of such ideas but frequently struggled against them.

References

1 Davidoff and Hall (1987), p. 13.
2 Strachey (1931), p. 177.
3 'Treatment of women', p. 225.
4 Davidoff and Hall (1987).
5 Purvis (1981a) and Purvis (1989) Chapter 3.
6 Lewis (1840, eighth edition), p. 56, first pub. 1839; Greg (1862), p. 339.
7 Ellis (1839), p. 149.
8 A Mother (1868), p. 91; Smiles (1884 new edition, first pub. 1871), p. 299.
9 Ellis (1842), p. 3; Ruskin (1865), p. 155.
10 Moore (1886), p. 31.
11 Ellis (1843), pp. 90–91.
12 *Enquire Within Upon Everything* (1898), p. 304.
13 Davidoff and Hall (1987), p. 322.
14 *Englishwoman's Review* 15 October 1877, p. 466.
15 Weeks (1981), p. 68.
16 Oakley (1976), p. 32, first pub. 1974.
17 Mayhew (1852), p. 263.
18 Ranyard (1859), p. 269.
19 Glendinning (1969), p. 9.
20 Quoted in Horn (1975), p. 59.
21 Gorham (1982), p. 11.
22 Quoted in Pinchbeck (1930), p. 315.
23 Bell (1942), p. 41.
24 Chorley (1950), p. 150.
25 See Davidoff (1973), p. 43.

26 Peel (1933), p. 95.
27 Burstyn (1980), pp. 74–5.
28 Booth (1855), p. 15.
29 Smiles (1859), p. 1.
30 Smiles (1843), p. 421.
31 Smiles (1871), p. 59.

CHAPTER 2

Education and Working-class Girls

During the period 1800–1914, a working-class girl might attend any of a range of educational institutions. These included dame schools (small private schools usually run by one woman or 'dame' in her own home), Sunday schools, charity schools, factory schools, ragged schools (free schools provided by philanthropists for children considered too dirty and poor to be acceptable elsewhere), the day schools run by the National Society for Promoting the Education of the Poor in the Principles of the Established Church (the Church of England) or the much smaller British and Foreign School Society (largely supported by religious dissenters) and day board schools founded after the 1870 Education Act.

Although the focus of this chapter will be upon the main institutions that working-class girls attended – dame schools, Sunday schools, National schools, British (and Foreign) schools and board schools – it is important not to forget that throughout the period under study, the working-class family itself could also be an important educational resource. In the early nineteenth century, Pole observed that the elderly instructing the young was 'a sight familiar to us all'.[1] And such an activity undoubtedly took place in a number of working-class homes throughout the period 1800–1914. In the Oxfordshire hamlet of Lark Rise in the 1880s, Laura (assumed to be a pseudonym for Flora Thompson), the daughter of humble rural folk, was taught to read by her parents before she attended the local school:

> their father brought home two copies of Mavor's First Reader and taught them the alphabet; but just as Laura was beginning on words of one syllable, he was sent away to work on a distant job, only

coming home at week-ends. Laura, left at the 'C-a-t s-i-t-s on the m-a-t' stage, had then to carry her book round after her mother as she went about her housework, asking: 'Please, Mother, what does h-o-u-s-e spell?' or 'W-a-l-k, Mother, what is that?' Often when her mother was too busy or too irritated to attend to her, she would sit and gaze on a page that might as well have been printed in Hebrew for all she could make of it, frowning and poring over the print as though she would wring out the meaning by force of concentration.

After weeks of this, there came a day when, quite suddenly, as it seemed to her, the printed characters took on a meaning. . . . 'I'm reading! I'm reading!' she cried aloud.[2]

Laura's parents had a few books in the house, unlike most other neighbouring families. For working-class girls, such books could be an indispensable aid that might compensate for a short time in, or indeed lack, of any 'formal' schooling. Indeed, the 1851 Census records that of the estimated total number of 9,146,384 females in the population of England and Wales, only 10.8 per cent attended day school.[3] In other words, by 1851 formal schooling was the experience of only a *minority* of working-class girls. Whether a working-class girl attended school or not was related to the material and domestic situation of her parents. During the first half of the nineteenth century in particular, working-class girls were likely to be engaged in paid work at an early age since the amount they could earn, however small, was necessary to supplement the family income. But in addition to this burden of their social class location, working-class girls also experienced the burden of their gender in that as girls, rather than boys, they were also expected to undertake a range of unpaid domestic duties considered an essential part of their 'femininity'.

Dame schools

Although the term 'dame school' has been applied to a range of infant schools for children in all social classes, it usually refers to those small, private venture schools opened by working-class women in their own homes. Sutherland claims that dames were primarily child minders, some of them ruthlessly exploiting a situation in which an increasing number of mothers went out to work.[4] Other historians offer a different interpretation. Gardner, for example, asserts that dame schools represented a genuine alternative working-class approach to childhood learning to that prescribed by middle-class 'experts'; while the experts decreed that education equals schools, the working-class private school operated on the assumption that education should permeate everyday living.[5] In its curriculum and mode of operation, the dame school bore a much closer relationship to the realities of working-class life than any school 'provided' by middle-class organizations, such as the National or the British and Foreign School Societies. Whereas the day schools of the religious societies attempted to impose strict rules about attendance and dress, the dame schools did not: here a working-class girl could attend irregularly *and* wear her long hair, without any fear of the dame demanding that it be cut short in order to prevent the spread of head lice.

In addition, the numerous, small dame schools, sometimes two operating in the same street, were also closer to home, warmer and more familial in atmosphere. And in many areas, as in those counties visited by the Rev. James Fraser, one of six assistant commissioners who reported to the Newcastle Commission in 1861, dames collected their pupils from the parental home. Furthermore, Fraser contended that it was the almost universal view of parents that children were taught to read quicker and better in dame schools than in the lower classes of the schools provided by middle-class philanthropists.[6] Factors such as these help to explain the popularity of dame schools with working-class parents who would often pay a weekly fee of fourpence to sixpence to a dame, rather than the few pence charged by the allegedly 'superior' church schools.

Dame school pupils were usually taught reading and perhaps also spelling, sewing and knitting. It is hard to determine whether a common curriculum was taught to both girls and boys but it would appear that for either sex, only basic knowledge was acquired, if any at all. At 'old Betty W's school' in Tunstall in the 1830s, beginners learnt the alphabet and then progressed to a reading-made-easy book with words in two, three or four letters. Once this was mastered, the next tasks were spelling and reading the Bible. Those successful in reading were offered special privileges, such as learning how to knit stockings – a reward open to both boys and girls.[7] Similarly, Mrs Sopps, a washerwoman and monthly nurse who also ran a village dame school in the 1850s was 'supposed' to teach reading, writing, summing and knitting to both boys and girls. She also taught both boys and girls the importance of 'bowing and curtsying to their betters',[8] a practice that was probably more prevalent in rural than the more cosmopolitan, urban areas where the influence of the church and local gentry was less strong. The one area of the curriculum that appears to have been taught to girls only in co-educational dame schools was sewing. The Rev. James Allen, for example, reported in the early 1840s that in nearly all the dame schools he visited in Derby girls learnt sewing.[9]

Gender differentiation in the curriculum was probably most pronounced in single sex dame schools. Mary Smith, born in 1822 in Cropredy, Oxfordshire, whose father was a boot and shoe maker, attended a girls only dame school when she was seven years old, solely for the purpose of learning to knit and sew. The woman who kept the school had an illness which prevented her from moving from her chair or lifting her arm to her mouth. However, she controlled her charges with a large white stick which reached to any part of the cottage floor. Mary recollects that the knowledge of the dame was 'very small'; though some reading was taught, knitting and sewing occupied nearly the whole time of the pupils.[10] Sewing was a practical skill considered particularly suitable for working-class girls. It could be utilized as unpaid work within the parental home, be part of vocational training for low paid women's work as a sewing woman, milliner or dressmaker, and also be a preparation for a future role as wife and mother.

The range of experiences for working-class girls in dame schools obviously varied. Some undoubtedly found a mother substitute, who offered care and affection; some learnt to read, and a few to write. Others, perhaps, were less fortunate and may have acquired only a few practical skills, such as sewing or knitting. But for all working-class girls, the meagre education of the dame school could be interrupted by domestic duties at home that were not expected of working-class boys. Ada Nield Chew, born in 1870 in North Staffordshire, whose father was a small farmer, had seven brothers and one sister, May, who was an epileptic. As the eldest daughter in such a large labouring family, her short attendance at the local dame school was an intermittent experience:

> Ada was . . . the only dependable daughter in a household where for many years there was a new baby every year, and her services became an indispensable adjunct to those of her mother. Boys were not expected to help with cooking, baking, cleaning, washing and the care of younger children, so Ada had to shoulder all these burdens

from an early age . . . She never went out to play without a baby
in her arms, never knew the joyous irresponsibility of more fortunate
children.[11]

By 1870, the year of Ada's birth, the state-aided day schools of the
National and British Societies had gained a hold on educational
provision for the working classes. Dame schools now attracted only
a minority of working-class children, although some of these institutions did survive into the twentieth century.[12] For the first half
of the nineteenth century in particular, the dame schools was an
important form of schooling for working-class girls that was often
combined with attendance at a Sunday school.

Sunday schools

Robert Raikes, who in the 1780s established Sunday schools for
poor children in Gloucester, is generally regarded as the founder of
the Sunday school movement. Though the motives of those who
established Sunday schools varied, the Sunday school movement in
its early years is generally seen as an attempt to rescue and save the
souls of children in the poorest strata of society by teaching them
to read the Bible and to abide by Christian principles.

In a study of Sunday schools from 1780–1850, Laqueur makes
the controversial suggestion that by the early nineteenth century
Sunday schools were not an imposition by the middle classes upon
the working classes, but a part of the working-class community.
Many of those who founded Sunday schools, he asserts, were from
the working class, and after 1810 some 60 per cent of all Sunday
schools teachers had once been students themselves.[13] Other
historians disagree with this analysis. For E.P. Thompson, Sunday
schools were a means whereby the middle classes attempted to
exercise class social control over the poor. Toddlers who were
taught to sing that they were 'By nature and by practice too, A
wretched slave to sin' were subjected, Thompson asserts, to a form
of indoctrination and bullying that made Sunday schools a 'dreadful
exchange even for village dame's schools.' Dick supports this view,
arguing that Sunday schools were evangelical and conservative
institutions, promoted and staffed by individuals from social classes
which were higher than those of the scholars who attended them,
and espousing an ideology which attacked the allegedly depraved
behaviour and radical inclinations of the poor. Furthermore,

although Sunday schools helped to create a culture of religion and respectability, which was absorbed by many working-class people, this culture was not solely of their own making. In Sunday-school instruction, Dick continues, qualities such as self-help and self-improvement were firmly associated with the deferential attitudes which Sunday schools tried to disseminate.[14]

While the debate continues, it is important not to forget that for working-class girls in the first half of the nineteenth century in particular, Sunday schools were an important form of part-time education – especially since, as stated earlier, only a minority of girls attended day schools. Indeed, it would appear that during the period 1834–43, the great majority of girls and boys in Sunday schools in the manufacturing centres of the North and the Midlands, the industrial and mining villages of the Forest of Dean, the West Riding, Staffordshire, Leicestershire or Lancashire received no other elementary education; half or nearly half of those receiving any education were receiving it on Sundays only.[15]

In the Sunday school, a working-class girl might learn to read and, if lucky, to write. The teaching of writing was a controversial issue, often seen as secular rather than religious instruction, and especially so by the Anglican church; consequently, writing was often confined to a weekday class. Nevertheless, a number of Sunday schools run by dissenting denominations did teach this skill. Samuel Bamford, a working-class radical, recollects that in early nineteenth century Lancashire, the Methodists of Middleton kept a Sunday school where both boys and girls sang hymns, said prayers and learnt how to spell and write. The day was a long one, beginning at half past eight in the morning and ending at 4 or half past. During the morning, the girls were taught in the gallery above, the boys in the room below. The school reassembled at 2, after the 1 o'clock service, when the girls occupied the writing desks in the downstairs room.[16]

To what extent girls and boys experienced a common curriculum is difficult to determine. Publications by the Religious Tract Society, such as *The Good Sunday Scholars*, exhorted both girls and boys to become good pupils who would attend punctually, prepare lessons at home, be attentive to what was taught and honour their parents. Furthermore:

GOOD SUNDAY SCHOLARS READ THE BIBLE AT HOME, love prayer, keep away from bad company, and are humble in spirit. By their good conduct, they are examples to other children. Yet they do not think that their own goodness will save their souls. They know they are sinners, and they ask God to give them his Holy Spirit to make them pure in heart and life.[17]

But other religious material contained many messages about the different and appropriate spheres for girls and boys, women and men, in Victorian society. Such messages may also have been reinforced by teacher expectations for their pupils.

Elementary textbooks used to teach pupils to read and write were primarily religious, many using extracts from Bible stories. The aim was to wean pupils from such textbooks as soon as possible so that they could then read the Bible or the New Testament: indeed, the percentage of pupils enrolled in reading the latter was taken as indicative of a Sunday school's 'efficiency or success'.[18] However, the Bible, in the main, portrays women as primarily wives and mothers who are inferior and subordinate to men. One wonders how the First Epistle of Paul the Apostle to the Corinthians was received by Sunday school pupils:

34. Let your women keep silence in the churches: for it is not permitted unto them to speak; but *they are commanded* to be under obedience, as also saith the law.
35. And if they will learn any thing, let them ask their husbands at home: for it is a shame for women to speak in the church.[19]

Other religious reading matter, which might be borrowed from a Sunday school library, given free or bought for a few pence, often contained similar gender messages about woman's position in society. Mary Anne Hearne, born in 1834 in Eynsford, Kent, whose father was a village postmaster, recollects that the Sunday School Union published in their magazines a series of articles on men who had been poor boys and risen to be rich and great: there was never, she bitterly complained, a woman in the whole series.[20] Whether the 'invisibility' of 'successful' women fired Mary Anne Hearne to aspire to greater things we do not know. But when a young woman she earned her living as a teacher and a writer, and in 1884 became the editor of *The Sunday School Times*. Throughout her unmarried life, the influence of her religion remained strong. She was a working-class girl for whom the Sunday school was a means of emotional comfort and support, as well as a means of social mobility.

By 1861, there were 1,210,297 female and 1,178,100 male Sunday scholars, making a total of nearly two and a half million.[21] By this time the number of adolescent girls and boys had increased, and continued to do so, for the rest of the nineteenth century. In Stockport in 1860, for example, the average age of entrants was 13 compared with 9.75 years in 1800.[22]

But other changes occurred too, well into the twentieth century; in particular, secular instruction began to diminish and religious instruction to become more systematic. The decline in the teaching of reading and writing was directly linked to the decline in the number of children employed in full-time paid work, the increase in the number of children in day schools and the advent of legislation from the 1870s to enforce compulsory school attendance.

As religious teaching became more systematic, there was a greater emphasis upon expounding and explaining the content of the Bible, including the parables. Such teaching probably rarely challenged the traditional division of labour between men and women and the social hierarchy between the social classes. Laura recollects that in an Oxfordshire hamlet in the 1880s, the themes of the church services were the same as those of her Sunday class:

> Mr Ellison in the pulpit was the Mr Ellison of the Scripture lessons, plus white surplus. To him, his congregation were but children of a larger growth, and he preached as he taught. A favourite theme was the duty of regular churchgoing . . . Another favourite subject was the supreme rightness of the social order as it then existed. God, in His infinite wisdom, had appointed a place for every man, woman, and child on his earth and it was their bounden duty to remain contentedly in their niches.[23]

Some children relieved the boredom of Sunday school lessons and church services by 'larking about'. As Stephen Humphries notes, since prayer was the most sacred and solemn religious ritual in which working-class children participated, it was also the most vulnerable to their profane and disruptive pranks.[24] Alice Hemmings, born in Bristol in 1898, whose father was a bakery boiler stoker, recollects that at one evening service, the boys tied the streamers on her hat to her chair; when she stood up, the chair came up with her – much to the annoyance of the Reverend Swann who asked those causing the disturbance to leave.[25]

Far more exciting for most Sunday scholars in the post 1850 era was the recreational role that both Church (Anglican) and Chapel (nonconformist) Sunday schools increasingly adopted. For Louisa

Hamer born in 1873, in Rawstenstall, Lancashire, the Sunday school was the centre of village life in the 1880s – 'We had no theatre, no picture house, no dance hall, no public library, no trams, no taxis . . . For entertainment well the Sunday Schools were "Tops" – bazaars, sales of work, bring and buys, American Teas, At homes and amateur operatic societies'.[26] Similarly, for Kate Edwards in the Lotting Fen district of Huntingdonshire, the Methodist Sunday School Anniversary in the 1880s and 1890s was an annual event for everyone, however poor, to appear well dressed and do their best:

> The last high day of the year, except for Ramsey Fair, were the Sunday School Anniversary. This were the child'en's very own day . . . The Sunday school teachers had been teaching 'em special hymns for weeks and between the hymns such children as dared and could learn their 'piece' said recitation or sung little hymns in pairs or even an occasional solo. It were a terrible ordeal to stand up facing all the people and 'say your piece'. We used to practice it for days and nights . . . Every mother, however poor she was, had to get her child'en looking smart for the anniversary, and if they couldn't buy new clothes for their families every child had to have one thing new. Among the girls, the secret o' what they were going to wear were kept as if their lives depended on it, and many a mother has dragged out to work for weeks in the field to be able to buy the new things for the anni.[27]

The time and effort put in by working-class mothers to enable their daughters to partake in such 'treats' continued into the twentieth century. Gladys Allsop, born in Manchester in 1907, regularly joined other Sunday school scholars in the Whit Monday Walks. One particular Whit Monday, when she was seven years old, her mother stayed up late on the preceding Saturday, making from a remnant of pure silk a dress 'larger than necessary' so that it would last longer; but it was the shepherd's crook decorated with flowers that she had to carry that made the occasion memorable.[28]

Although Charles Booth, a Victorian middle-class social reformer, is alleged to have said that working-class parents sent their children to Sunday school in order to have a free afternoon for sexual intercourse without fear of being disturbed, there are other factors to consider! During the first half of the nineteenth century in particular, the Sunday school, in comparison with other forms of schooling, had two key advantages for poor parents – it was free and therefore involved no extra outlay and it was held on a day which might not interfere with a daughter's paid work. For the working-class daughter who had no access to any other form of education, a Sunday school could offer a limited education. Indeed, Laqueur argues that the three to five hours' instruction each week, for an average of four years, had a major impact on the creation of mass literacy.[29] However, throughout the period 1800–1914, the literacy rate of women was persistently below that of men. For the working-class girl schooled only in those 'inferior' forms of education, such as dame or Sunday schools, with few chances in later life to improve or retain those basic educational skills acquired, being 'literate' would always be a problem.

Weekday schools

The two main providers of weekday schools in nineteenth-century England were the British and Foreign Society and the National Society, founded in 1808 and 1811, respectively. By 1870, these two bodies were providing over 90 per cent of voluntary school places.[30] The Church of England National Society was especially influential, even by the beginning of the twentieth century. Thus it has been estimated that in 1895 6.2 per cent of all elementary schools in England and Wales were with the British and Foreign Society, 24.2 per cent were connected with the school boards created by the 1870 Education Act and 61.6 per cent were with the National Society: the Anglican schools were especially numerous in agricultural counties, such as Lincolnshire, where they comprised 71.7 per cent of the total.[31] In 1833, the two religious societies had attracted government grants to help with the erection of school buildings. Over the course of the nineteenth century, the amount of aid not only increased but the range of grants multiplied. Consequently, National and British schools carried the stigma of 'charity' and were seen as an 'imposition' upon working-class life, and 'provided' by the middle classes.

The aims of the two religious societies were not just to impart basic knowledge and religious instruction but also to instil certain habits and manners considered appropriate for the 'lower' orders. The aims of the National Society, stated in its *First Annual Report* in 1812, were to communicate to the poor such knowledge and habits as were sufficient to guide them through life 'in their proper stations, especially to teach the doctrines of Religion, according to the principles of the Established Church and to train them to the performance of their religious duties by early discipline'.[32] What becomes clear is that the proper station in life for working-class girls was considered to be a domestic location within the home, usually as a 'good' servant and then as a 'good' wife and mother. Thus by 1841, the National Society stipulated that female pupils should be taught 'to be sober, to love their husbands, to love their children, to be discreet, chaste, keepers at home, obedient to their husbands that the word of God be not blasphemed'.[33] Similarly, the Ladies' Committee of the British Society noted in the Society's *Reports* for 1822 and 1833 that working-class girls should ideally be taught 'useful knowledge' that would qualify them to become 'industrious servants' who would one day be 'the wives and mothers of industrious and intelligent mechanics'.[34]

The experience of schooling for working-class girls in National and British schools was likely therefore to be sharply different from that in dame and Sunday schools. Sexual divisions between girls and boys, for example, were much more *formalized* – especially in comparison with the more haphazard arrangements in many dame schools. Thus one could find single sex schools and also mixed sex schools with separate entrances, sections, departments or rooms for boys and girls. At the Central Schools in London of the National Society, for example, we find separate rooms for boys and girls.[35] At Watton, Norfolk, in 1845 we find a more common arrangement – the boys and girls were taught in the same large room but in separate divisions.[36] Single sex schools were more likely to be found in urban areas where the larger population could support such a venture. Village schools, in contrast, were more likely to include both sexes – and all ages.

The separate divisions between girls and boys were perhaps most pronounced in regard to curricula. At the National Society's Central Schools both boys and girls were taught the same subjects in the morning – prayers, ciphering, religious' exercises, writing and reading – but in the afternoon, the girls did needlework and knitting till half past four and then arithmetic till five o'clock, while the boys continued with ciphering, writing, reading and arithmetic.[37] Similarly the British schools offered both boys and girls the 3Rs and religious knowledge with needlework only for girls.[38]

For the first twenty years of their existence, the National and British schools centred their teaching on the Scriptures. However, radicals, professional educationalists, churchmen, government inspectors and leaders within the religious societies began increasingly to question the wisdom of this practice. In 1843, the Rev. Edward Feild, a National Society Inspector, asserted that he found 'an increasing conviction' that it was 'right and necessary' to introduce more books of secular and general knowledge into the schools.[39] By 1850, secular readers, often grudgingly, had replaced many of the 'old' religious texts. By this time too other subjects, such as history and geography, might also be taught – especially in the London-based 'model' schools (those schools which also offered teacher training) of the National and British Societies.

To what extent working-class girls in other parts of the country participated in all of these new developments is difficult to determine. Although the Rev F.C. Cook claimed in the early 1840s that geography was now taught in most National schools, he also regretted that the subject had encountered 'much opposition on the part of some excellent persons' when introduced into several girls' schools.[40] Undoubtedly there were some schools, other than the 'model' schools where girls did have access to a wider curriculum. The National girls' school at Norwich, for example, offered elementary subjects, geography, English history, grammar, etymology, domestic economy, marching and singing.[41] But overall, it would appear that by 1850 that minority of working-class girls who did attend National and British schools were still experiencing a basic grounding in the 3Rs, religious knowledge and sewing. The absence of maps and the relevant textbooks often made the teaching of 'new' subjects difficult, even if teachers were willing. In addition, during the first half of the nineteenth century in particular, there was another important factor that would have limited the educational opportunities of working-class girls, a monitorial method of teaching.

The monitorial system relied upon older pupils or 'monitors' (frequently 8 to 11 years old) teaching younger pupils in a mechanistic way. Under this system, one teacher would have responsibility for the efficient management of the large single schoolroom and for training the monitors. Joseph Lancaster of the British Society along with Andrew Bell of the National Society are usually credited with being the 'inventors' of the method. Lancaster, for example, organized his school of 1000 pupils at Borough Road in this way; the sole teacher there, he employed and trained sixty-seven monitors.

As Sturt has observed, under the monitorial teaching method, everything was reduced to its basic elements.[42] Reading, for example, began with making letters in sand while the monitor watched carefully; then the spelling and writing of two-letter syllables would begin. Once this was mastered, the pupil 'progressed' to the next grade or class. Chanting of dates, verses from the Bible and other set replies were common. The great advantage of the method was that it was cheap. There was only the salary of the teacher to be paid, plus a small fee to the monitors of usually not more than 6d. weekly – although in some cases no payment was made at all.[43]

The fact that monitors were often poorly educated children themselves who had difficulty controlling their charges, plus the mechanistic replies that their 'teaching' encouraged, held important implications for the way schooling was experienced. Endless repetition of 'set' replies undoubtedly occurred until each class provided, or appeared to provide, the correct answer. Many children must have copied each other, aped words that were similar to the expected answer and misunderstood the lesson content. In 1840 the Rev. Baptist W. Noel inspected elementary schools in Birmingham, Liverpool, and several other towns in Lancashire; his comments on one particular girls' school are not untypical:

> Thirty-one girls read . . . to their monitor. The noise in the school was so great that as I sat by the monitor I could not hear the girl who was reading in the class. Several children were laughing to each other, others were inattentive; and the only symptom of reverence in the whole class was, that every time the name of our Lord was pronounced the whole class made a short rapid courtsey, occasioning along the whole class an irregular popping down, the effect of which, combined with their undisguised levity, was exceedingly unpleasant.[44]

In 1845 another inspector, the Rev Frederick Watkins, complained that monitors 'took no notice of the children working and knitting during prayers. None of the girl-teachers could do a sum in compound multiplication which they professed'.[45]

The government could not ignore such persistent criticisms; it increased the level of financial support for teacher training granted to the National and British Societies and also became active itself in training provision. In 1846, a pupil-teacher system was created whereby a five-year, grant-aided, pupil-teacher apprenticeship could be offered to pupils of either sex who had completed elementary schooling of a satisfactory standard up to the age of 13. Although such a scheme, together with other initiatives, helped to develop professional awareness amongst elementary schoolteachers, the quality of classroom life, especially from the pupil's point of view, was constrained by another reform – the Revised Code of 1862.

The government was becoming concerned about the increasing amount of grant being given to elementary education for the working classes and thus Robert Lowe, Vice-President of the Education Department, introduced a system of 'Payment by Results', inaugurated in the Revised Code of 1862. Under this system, all future grants, apart from building, were to be made on the basis of a payment of 12s. per child per annum – which could only be earned under certain conditions. Four shillings could be earned for regular attendance at a school (run by a qualified headteacher) while the rest of the money could only be awarded if a satisfactory standard was attained in the 3Rs examination now conducted by Her Majesty's Inspectorate. If a pupil failed in any one of the 3Rs, two shillings and eightpence was deducted from that pupil's grant. The examinations were graded and each child was expected to pass the annual test and move yearly up to the next standard. In addition, for girls only, plain needlework remained an examinable obligatory subject.

Such reforms embodied the first attempt to implement a core or national curriculum for working-class pupils in state aided elementary schools. Furthermore, the subordination of the curriculum to a test procedure encouraged rather than diminished certain aspects of the monitorial system – such as rote learning, chanting, recitation and drilling. As Christina Bremner complained in 1897, the main faults of schools before 1870 were the 'dull, soulless, monotony, parrot-like repetition, mechanical grinding'.[46] From 1867, a higher grant could be earned if extra 'specific' subjects, such as geography and history, were taught and in 1871 the list was extended to include algebra, geometry, natural philosophy, physical geography, the natural sciences, political economy and languages, together with any other subject approved by the HMI: about the same time, drill and singing were also encouraged.[47] But the number of working-class girls who had access to this broader curriculum was likely to be small; in 1875 only 3.7 per cent of all elementary pupils were examined in any of the specific subjects.[48]

The Code of 1900 abolished all piecemeal grants and schools now received capitation grants of 17s. for each infant and 22s. for each older child. Even though this ended the 'payment by results' system, old teaching methods lingered on – and also a narrow curriculum, especially in rural areas. Hilda Winstanley, born in 1896, and brought up by a labouring family in a village fourteen miles from Manchester, attended the local Church of England day school. The examination by the local Inspector in 1909 included none of the newer subjects but the old favourites of arithmetic, spelling, history, geography and essay writing. And the terror of the annual examination remained the same for pupils and teachers under the Revised Code as it did now for 'our 'ilda' and her teacher, Miss Holroyd. Thus the cross-examination conducted by the Inspector regarding the spelling in Hilda's essay on 'The Royal Family' caused much anxiety to both pupil and teacher:

> The Inspector . . . beckoned Hilda to the blackboard and told her to write 'The Prince of Wales'. Hilda, puzzled, and with Miss Holroyd looking beseechingly at her, took up the chalk and wrote boldly:
> 'The Prince of Whales'.
> The Inspector again looked at Miss Holroyd, and then asked Hilda to look at what she had written carefully, and to write underneath it 'The Princess of Wales', and Hilda, now shaking with apprehension, again wrote, but less boldly:
> 'The Princess of Whales'.
> Miss Holroyd, her face burning, was in tears, and turning crossly to Hilda the Inspector asked: 'In what country is Caernarvon situated?'
> 'In the country of Wales', stammered Hilda.
> 'Right', said the Inspector. 'Now write on the blackboard – Caernarvon is in the country of Wales.'
> Hilda, her fingers shaking so that she could scarcely guide the chalk, wrote:
> 'Caenarvon is in the country of Wales'.
> The Inspector's face lightened, and so did Miss Holroyd's.
> 'Now, child, tell me what made you write the first Wales with an "h"?'
> Hilda, red with shame, and instantly perceiving the stupid mistake, answered miserably: 'I don't know, Sir. I've never written it that road before. I don't know what made me do it'. She began to cry, but the Inspector patted her shoulder kindly and laughed.[49]

Hilda was at a National school and such schools still existed in the early twentieth century since the 1870 Education Act did not abolish the National and British day schools, but supplemented them. Thus the Act specified that in districts which lacked efficient and suitable provision for elementary education, a school board should be established to rectify the deficiency. The new board schools were intended for working-class children (though some children from the lower middle class did attend them) and not seen as a stepping stone to secondary education.

Up to 1914, the state became increasingly involved in financing and controlling elementary schooling. The age of 'compulsory' school attendance, for example, was raised to ten, eleven and fourteen in 1880, 1893 and 1899, respectively, though exceptions were allowed for part-time working under local bye-laws. In 1918, the half time system ended, and fourteen became the uniform compulsory school leaving age. From 1870 to 1914, the state also increased the number of grants for certain subjects taught in elementary schools (whether British, National or board schools) and supported scholarship schemes for entry to secondary education. Both of these measures, however, sharpened even further the already existing sexual divisions between working-class schoolgirls and schoolboys.

Expansion of grants for domestic subjects

The Education Department influenced the elementary curriculum through the provision of grants, and for working-class girls the influence was in the direction of an *expansion* of domestic subjects. After domestic economy was made a compulsory specific subject for girls in 1878, grants were made in 1882 for the teaching of cookery and in 1890 for laundry work. As Dyhouse notes, the impact of these measures was impressive; in 1882–3, 7,597 girls from a total of 457 schools had qualified for the cookery grant and by 1885–6 these numbers had risen to 134,930 and 2,729, respectively. Between 1891–2 and 1895–6, the number of girls taking recognized classes in laundry work similarly rose from 632 to 11,720 – the number of schools offering these classes increasing from 27 to 400.[50] The textbooks for use in schools at this time made it quite clear that the 'new' subjects should involve the learning of useful, practical skills *and* character training. Margaret Rankin, for example, gave the following 'hint' to those women teachers using her textbook on the art and practice of laundry work:

There is nothing more likely to aid in the development of character in children than the thorough inculcation of this science of cleanliness . . . While guiding the pupils into methodical ways of working, . . . [the teacher will] also influence the character of the pupils by the formation of habits such as punctuality, cleanliness, tidiness, carefulness, and order.[51]

Such habits were, of course, to prepare working-class schoolgirls to become *good women*, capable and efficient wives and mothers – who could do all their own housework and organize their homes in a competent manner. Such messages were frequently stated in the school textbooks, as in the 1896 popular *Longmans' Domestic Economy Readers for Standards VI and VII* which told girls 'first to be good Home Managers, planning your work well, and carrying out your plans' and then to be 'Home Geniuses, taking infinite pains over all that you do'.[52] Encouragement to be a 'Home Genius' did not entail academic achievement but mastery of low-status, practical skills. As Davin observes, elementary textbooks which presented girls and women in their 'natural' sphere of the home directed schoolgirls towards an exclusively domestic role, even at the expense of scholastic achievement.[53]

In 1900, a grant of 7s. was offered for every girl in Standard V and above who had attended a course of eighty to one hundred hours' instruction in household management, which was to be interpreted as a combined course in cookery, laundry work and housewifery.[54] Pressure also grew to teach infant care to all elementary schoolgirls over twelve years of age. After much debate about the issue, a Board of Education Circular issued in 1910 recommended that infant care should not be taught as an isolated subject but as part of an integrated course in hygiene and household management. Many elementary schoolteachers undoubtedly interpreted the recommendations in the expected manner, although some adopted an unorthodox method. Miss Outram, headmistress at Dronfield Elementary School, Derbyshire, included in her 1913 course on domestic economy and home management not only basic ante-natal care but also discussion of circumcision and infertility. A eugenist and feminist (she had read to her girls extracts from *The Suffragette*) she caused a scandal in the close knit community when later that year she gave some sex education teaching as part of scripture lessons. Distraught parents complained that school education should not include such 'disgusting and abominable information'.[55]

Writers such as Anna Davin, Annmarie Turnbull, Miriam David and Carol Dyhouse link the expansion in domestic subjects for elementary schoolgirls to fears about the future of the British race and the decline of the British Empire.[56] The call-up for the Boer War (1899–1902) had revealed that large numbers of potential male recruits were physically unfit for service. In addition, a falling birth rate coupled with a high infant mortality rate aroused concern about the quality of maternal care and the quantity of potential recruits for the defence of the Empire. The much debated Report of the Inter-Departmental Committee on Physical Deterioration (1904) contained numerous statements by the middle class about the low standard of living amongst the poor in congested urban areas. In particular, witnesses to the committee emphasized the 'inadequacies' of the working-class wife. Since children were seen as 'a national asset', 'the citizens of tomorrow',[57] it was believed critical to 'educate' working-class, elementary schoolgirls for wifehood and motherhood. The results, however, were not always as anticipated by government officials.

Many of the working-class women interviewed by Elizabeth Roberts about their lives in three Lancashire towns in the late nineteenth and early twentieth century stated that school domestic science was 'never any help'. Mrs Hewitson, born in 1885, a pupil at Rawlinson Street School, Barrow, remembered taking home dirty-looking scones which none of her family wanted to eat; similarly, the collars she had to wash, starch and iron in laundry lessons were promptly re-washed by her mother.[58] Grace Foakes, who spent her childhood in East London around the turn of the nineteenth century, found that the school housewifery course, held in a house set aside for the purpose, was the highlight of the week since while the busy teacher was inspecting another part of the house, the girls 'jumped on the bed, threw pillows, drowned the doll and swept dirt under the mats'.[59] Kate Taylor, born in Pakenham, Suffolk, in 1891, the fourteenth of fifteen children of an agricultural labourer, went to a local school where the headmaster's wife who taught needlework would never allow her pupils 'to do anything worthwhile':

Oddments of wool to knit, unknit and reknit – the same with needle-work, just odds and ends to stitch together, unpick and restitch. One afternoon, after taking the same little piece of calico, sewn, unsewn and resewn for the sixth time, I just threw it on her desk, jumped the seat, through the door, jumped the playground wall, and was away home.[60]

Overall, it would appear that for many working-class girls, it was their mothers' training at home that was valued rather than the 'unreal' situations created in schools. As Turnbull notes, the teaching of domestic subjects to working-class schoolgirls was fraught with difficulties and made little impact on the practical household skills of the nation.[61]

Scholarship system

The increased emphasis upon sexual divisions between boys and girls from 1870–1914 was evident also in the 'scholarship system' whereby poor elementary pupils could be offered a free place in a fee-paying secondary school. Although the number of scholarships was severely limited, more were offered to boys than to girls and this was especially so after the Technical Instruction Act of 1889 enabled counties and county boroughs to make grants to secondary schools for scholarship purposes. In Somerset in 1892, for example, the county council decided to found sixty-six 'County Scholarships' for boys, to be tenable for three years at a school within or adjoining the county, approved by the educational committee of the county as giving efficient technical instruction; no mention is made of scholarships for girls.[62] Similarly, Mrs Kitchener stated in her evidence to the Bryce Commission of 1895 (its object was to consider the best methods of establishing a well-organized system of secondary education in England) that in Lancashire, 'girls are far less well off' in the local authority scholarship schemes.[63] In addition to this handicap, working-class girls might also find that both their parents and teachers discriminated against them when they had scholastic ambitions for secondary schooling.

It would seem that those working-class parents who considered secondary schooling for their children, gave preference to their sons. Nora Lumb, born in 1912, whose father was a railway clerk, found that her parents would 'have paid for a boy, but not for a girl' to attend grammar school: Nora's only chance came in 1923 when she successfully competed for one of the ten scholarships awarded by Sunderland.[64] Ellen Wilkinson, born in 1891, won a series of scholarships that eventually enabled her to attend Manchester University. She bitterly recollects that in her 'filthy elementary school . . . with five classes in one room' the masters would 'often give extra time, lend books and so on to a bright lad. I never remembered such encouragement. I was only a girl anyway'.[65] Working-class scholarship girls, such as Ellen, were likely to find themselves in a minority amongst scholarship girls generally. Clara Collet, for example, found this to be so in London in 1892. Rather than enabling workmen to send their daughters to secondary school, the scholarship system, she asserted, encouraged middle-class men to send their daughters to board schools in the hope of winning a free place.[66]

For that small number of able scholarship girls from the 'lower orders', life at the 'new' school was not always happy. Annie Wilson, born to poor parents in Nottingham in 1898, won a free place from her board school in Bath Street to the fee-paying Huntingdon Street School. The snobbishness of her new school extended to the cloakroom where another girl threw Annie's hat off the cloakroom peg complaining 'I'm not going to put mine with the dirty Bath Street lot'.[67] Another working-class scholarship girl was 'socially ostracized in a fairly thorough manner . . . to the extent of being regularly ignored in the railway carriage on the way to school'.[68] Such behaviour could only isolate, rather than integrate, the working-class girl into her new surroundings.

In some areas, and especially in London, scholarships were offered for entry into vocational, junior technical or trade schools. And here, yet again, gender divisions between boys and girls were stoutly maintained. The trade schools for boys were designed to give 'specialized training that would fit them to enter about the age of 16 into workshop or factory life with a certain definite prospect of becoming skilled workers or of rising ultimately to positions of responsibility as foremen, draughtsmen, or even managers': the Trade School for Furniture and Cabinet-Making founded at the Shoreditch Technical Institute in 1901 was the first of such schools in London.[69] For girls, on the other hand, ten domestic service and eighteen domestic economy schools had been established by 1914 – four of the former type of school and twelve of the latter being in the London area. At the London domestic servants' schools, girls were admitted between the age of 13½ and 15 and trained for two years, with London County Council (LCC) scholarships offered to some pupils. LCC scholarships were also available for the laundry trade school, established by 1909 for girls aged 14 years of age and for the trade classes for girls, in subjects such as waistcoat making, dressmaking, ladies' tailoring and upholstery, organized at Borough Polytechnic:[70] As Horn notes, despite the apparent even-handedness of the Education Department Codes in ensuring that both male and female pupils were instructed in the 3Rs and, especially after 1900, in such 'extras' as history and geography, the reality was different; a clear domestic bias was applied to the girls' schooling.[71]

Why did mass schooling arise?

By 1914, a state system for mass elementary schooling had evolved. But why and how can we account for it? Historians tend to offer three main explanations. First, it is argued that Britain needed an educated electorate after the extension of political enfranchisement (in the late 1860s) to working-class men. Second, it is also stated that Britain needed an educated, skilled workforce who would produce goods for a competitive international market as well as home consumption. However, Anna Davin points out that while such explanations may help to account for the schooling of working-class boys, they hold no relevance for working-class girls since women did not have the right to vote in the nineteenth century and neither could they enter the range of skilled jobs which (it was believed) would bring economic prosperity.[72] A third explanation for the rise of mass schooling has been particularly advanced by Marxist historians who argue that education was seen by the middle classes as a means of reforming, civilizing and controlling a 'decadent' working class. Such Marxist explanations do not, however, consider gender divisions, although a fourth explanation does. Thus feminist historians, such as Davin and Dyhouse, argue that mass schooling was an attempt to impose upon working-class children a middle-class family form of a male breadwinner and an economically dependent wife and mother.[73] Such a family form would benefit all the family members – and the wider society. A wife at home full time could organize efficiently her household and provide a range of unpaid services to her husband and family. Such a 'stable' unit would provide a secure environment for the rearing of healthy children, the future workforce, and for the care and comfort of the male wage-earner.

References

1 Pole (1816), p. 62.
2 Thompson (1954), p. 32, first pub. 1945.
3 Quoted in Purvis (1989), p. 76.
4 Sutherland (1971), p. 12.
5 Gardner (1984), p. 4.
6 Quoted in Leinster-MacKay (1976), pp. 38–9.
7 Shaw (1903, 1977 reprint), pp. 2–3.
8 Marshall (1947), p. 2.
9 Committee of Council on Education, *Minutes 1841–2*, p. 260.
10 Smith (1892), pp. 24–5.
11 Chew (1982), p. 9.
12 See Gardner (1984), Chapter 7.
13 Laqueur (1976), p. 189.
14 Thompson (1972, first pub. 1963), pp. 413–14; Dick (1980), p. 36.
15 Laqueur (1976), p. 100.
16 Dunckley ed. (1893), Vol. 1, p. 101.
17 *The Good Sunday Scholars* (n.d.), pp. 7–8.
18 Laqueur (1976), p. 214.
19 *1 Corinthians*, Chapter 14.
20 Farningham (1907), p. 44.
21 *PP 1861 XXI, I*, pp. 592–3.
22 Laqueur (1976), p. 100.
23 Thompson (1954), p. 229.
24 Humphries (1981), pp. 132–3.
25 Ibid., p. 133.
26 Hamer (1967), p. 10.
27 Marshall (ed.), 1980, p. 206.
28 Allsop (1987), p. 7.
29 Laqueur (1976), p. 123.
30 Hurt (1979), p. 4.
31 Quoted in Horn (1974), p. 133.
32 National Society, *First Annual Report* (1812), p. 18.
33 Quoted in Gomersal (1988), p. 43.
34 British Society, *Report 1822*, p. 76 and *Report 1833*, p. 8.
35 National Society, *Second Annual Report* (1814), p. 194.
36 *PP 1845 XXXV*, p. 78.
37 National Society, *Second Annual Report* (1814), p. 195.
38 See Purvis (1981b), p. 107–8.
39 Quoted in Goldstrom (1977), p. 101.
40 *PP 1845 XXV*, pp. 66, 72.
41 Ibid., p. 80.
42 Sturt (1967), p. 31.

43 Central Society of Education (1837), p. 28.
44 Committee of Council on Education, *Minutes 1840–41*, p. 185.
45 Quoted in Horn (1978), p. 46.
46 Bremner (1897), p. 40.
47 Birchenough (1914), pp. 301–2.
48 Horn (1978), p. 126.
49 Penn (1979, facsimile edition of original first pub. 1947), pp. 125–6.
50 Dyhouse (1981), pp. 89–90.
51 Rankin (n.d., c. 1900), p. 9.
52 *Longmans' Domestic Economy Readers For Standards VI and VII* (1896), pp. 2–3.
53 Davin (1979), p. 98.
54 Sillitoe (1933), p. 35.
55 Quoted in Mort (1987), p. 158.
56 Davin (1978), Turnbull (1980), David (1980) and Dyhouse (1981).
57 Quoted in Davin (1978), p. 10.
58 Roberts (1984), pp. 32–3.
59 Foakes (1976), p. 47.
60 Taylor (1982), p. 290.
61 Turnbull (1987), p. 99.
62 Hobhouse (1892), p. 99.
63 Royal Commission on Secondary Education (Bryce Commission), *PP 1895 Vol. XLVIII*, p. 290.
64 Quoted in Burnett (1982), p. 163.
65 Wilkinson (1938), pp. 407, 404.
66 Collet (1892), p. 213.
67 Wilson (1981), p. 93.
68 Sokoloff (1987), p. 20.
69 Board of Education (1926), p. 32.
70 Horn (1988), p. 75.
71 Ibid., p. 76.
72 Davin (1979), p. 89.
73 Ibid. and Dyhouse (1981).

CHAPTER 3

'Good Wives and Mothers': Educational Provision for Working-class Women

Social class and gender differentiation, strongly evident in the forms and content of education for working-class girls, also structured and shaped that educational provision offered to working-class women during the Victorian and Edwardian eras. In particular, in those educational programmes organized by the middle classes we see a continuation of that class-specific, domestic ideal of femininity upheld for working-class girls – that of *good women* who would learn the 3Rs and practical domestic skills that might prepare them to become *good wives and mothers*. However, as we shall see, although such ideals were pervasive, other and competing ideals of femininity were also apparent.

Adult Sunday schools

The first Sunday school exclusively for adults was established for young working-class women employed in the lace and hosiery industries in Nottingham. In 1798, William Singleton, a Methodist, helped by Samuel Fox, a Quaker tradesman, opened an adult Sunday school for Bible reading and instruction in writing and arithmetic. Before long, the class became mainly organized by Fox, in his grocer's shop. All the shop assistants, mainly female, helped as teachers. A men's class was soon added.[1] Although the foundation of this school seems to have been a relatively isolated incident, a number of features of the school were replicated in future adult Sunday schools, i.e. the establishment of such schools as the result of middle-class initiative, especially that of businessmen; the involvement of nonconformist religious groups, especially the Quakers; separate provision for the sexes; a narrow curriculum that offered an introduction to literacy, and an emphasis upon using the Bible and other religious material as reading texts.

It was from Bristol, however, rather than Nottingham, that the adult Sunday school developed. In 1811, William Smith, 'a poor, humble, and almost unlettered individual, in Bristol, occupying no higher rank than that of a door-keeper to a methodist chapel', conceived the idea of instructing the adult poor to read the holy scriptures.[2] In February 1812, he contacted the Quaker Stephen Prust, a 'very respectable merchant'[3] who gave him every encouragement. By 1813, nine schools for men and nine for women had been established and by 1815, adult Sunday schools could be found in at least 20 towns in England.[4]

The American-born Quaker physician, Dr Thomas Pole, expressed the hopes of many middle-class commentators when in 1813 he stated that the benefits of adult Sunday schools extended beyond the individuals instructed to those within their own household. Adult Sunday scholars would learn industry, frugality, and economy and how to improve the practice of meekness, Christian fortitude and resignation. 'Is it not of consequence', questioned Pole, 'to make nominal Christians, better husbands – better wives – better parents – better children?'[5] An 1831 report revealed, yet again, how it was hoped that adult Sunday schools would 'reform' and 'civilize' working-class families:

> It must be extremely gratifying to the Conductors and Teachers of this Society, to find persons in their humble cottages reading the Bible with meditation and prayer, and thanking God that they ever attended an Adult School. Formerly they spent their Sabbaths in lounging, in walking in the fields for pleasure, in vain conversation, or in public houses; now they attend the public worship of Almighty God, wait at the posts of wisdom's doors, and receive instructions in the way of righteousness.[6]

As examples like this make clear, the aim of adult Sunday schools was not only teaching the poor to read the Bible but also a means of social class control. The culturally and morally 'deficient' working classes could be 'improved' by teaching them a different set of standards. In particular, working-class women, through learning Christian virtues, would become 'good' wives and mothers whose household skills would benefit the whole society.

In addition to this attempt to change their way of life, some working-class women might also find that their menfolk objected to their wives becoming literate. Thus one women who had attended one of the Bath adult schools was roughly treated by her seafaring husband who threatened to 'break her bones' if she continued her lessons.[7] Although not all working-class women experienced such opposition, we do find, as we shall later see, some recorded instances of such a gender struggle within the family. Many more examples are undoubtedly lost in history.

Despite the growing literacy rates in nineteenth-century England, adult schools continued to flourish and enjoyed a revival in the 1890s. By 1909–10 the movement had peaked to over 1,900 schools with over 100,000 students; by 1914 there were still nearly the same number of schools with over 80,000 students, of whom 42 per cent were women. Bible study continued to be the main feature of the work and the classes were still mainly held on Sundays, the men meeting in the morning, the women in the afternoon.[8] That the adult school survived for so long was due, claims Kelly, to their responsive to changing conditions. Although literacy classes were still a part of the curriculum, writing being taught up to 1914, the adult schools now functioned much more as 'societies' with a wide range of social and educational activities e.g. lectures, classes, discussions, study circles on weekday evenings and lecture schools at the weekends. A number of the adult schools became affiliated to the Workers' Educational Association (WEA), founded in 1903, and also developed links with the University Extension Movement, established in the late 1860s to offer part-time education to adults.[9] However, both of these later developments were not specifically aimed at working-class women. As we shall see in Chapter 5, the University Extension Movement partly arose in response to the demands of middle-class women and failed to attract their working-class sisters while the WEA was an association to promote the 'Higher Education of Working Men'.

Mechanics' institutes

The major adult education movement of the nineteenth century, however, was the mechanics' institute movement, which began in the 1820s. The aim of the institutes were both class and sex specific, i.e. the diffusion of scientifically useful knowledge to working-class men. As Duppa stated in 1839, 'The class of persons for whom Mechanics' Institutions were originally designed was, as the name indicates, Mechanics or Workmen'.[10] The institutes, as originally planned, were not intended to include women and thus women who wanted to study there had to fit into an educational movement for men. Consequently, women had to struggle to enter the mechanics' institutes and were admitted from 1830 onwards, somewhat reluctantly. At the London Mechanics' Institution, for example, the decision made in June 1830 to admit women who were relatives and friends of members to the lectures and circulating library was made against 'great opposition', the fear being expressed that such a decision would bring the institute into 'very great dispute' and lead to the admission of women of 'a very questionable character'.[11] It is no surprise to find that when women were admitted, they did not enjoy equality of membership or equality of treatment. Their subordinate status within the wider society was reflected in their marginal status within the institutes.

By 1841, 261 mechanics' institutes are recorded as existing, the largest concentration – about 22 per cent – being in the West Riding and Lancashire.[12] It is difficult to give an exact number of the total female membership since the necessary records do not always exists. Tylecote estimates that by 1849 there were 1200 women in the Yorkshire institutes and about half that number in Lancashire; I have calculated that in England and Wales in 1851 there were 5,710 women and 55,239 men members of mechanics' institutes, the women forming 9.4 per cent of the total membership.[13] Even more problematic is trying to establish the social class background of these women since the necessary information is not always recorded.

From the records that do exist it would appear that the institutes generally failed to attract large numbers of working-class women, just as they failed to attract the mass of unskilled male workers for whom they were intended. Since weekly subscriptions of 1d., 1½d. or 2d. (rather than half yearly fees of, say, 2s. or 3s. or annual fees of 5s. or 6s.) are usually a reliable indication of working-class background, working-class women were most likely to be found in those institutes operating such a scheme, i.e. the small, mixed sex institutes in the north of England and the two large women-only institutes in Huddersfield and Bradford. Thus it was claimed in 1847 that the membership of the small mixed sex Holbeck Institute included 'ignorant factory girls' who had been trained for Sunday school teaching.[14] At the Huddersfield Female Educational Institute, founded in 1847, the students were mainly milliners, dressmakers, domestic servants or women living at home with their parents.[15] The Bradford Female Educational Institute drew upon a similar clientele – spinners, weavers and other factory workers being the largest occupational groupings in the early 1860s.[16] This institute attracted nearly double the number of women members found at Huddersfield; thus in 1861, 473 students are recorded at the former but only 249 at the latter.[17]

Within the mixed sex institutes, two main tendencies shaped the organization of the teaching. Men and women were organized mainly in single sex groupings for class work but in regard to lectures, the sexes could attend together and, indeed, were expected to do so. Sex-segregated class teaching held important implications for the content of education since women and men were offered a *different* rather than a common curriculum. In particular, in most mixed sex institutes working-class women only had access to a narrow curriculum of reading, writing, arithmetic, plain sewing and some limited general knowledge while their menfolk were offered a much wider range of subjects. At Holmfirth during 1846–47, women were limited to the 3Rs, sewing and knitting while the men could attend classes in the 3Rs and general knowledge, the latter offering a range of topics such as the atmosphere, geology, China, electricity, galvanism, the properties of water, electrotype and phrenology.[18] At Lockwood Mechanics' Institute, Yorkshire, in 1857, the 212 male members could receive instruction in reading, writing, arithmetic, algebra, mensuration, history, geography, grammar, music, freehand and ornamental drawing while the choices offered to the 45 female members were restricted to reading, writing, arithmetic, knitting, sewing and marking.[19] When joint classes were held in an institute, it was mainly for recreational activities, such as singing.

Although it is not clear from the records why class teaching was organized in this way, it would appear that the institute organizers believed that women and men had different educational needs. Men's education was advocated in terms of its vocational value. Thus the introduction of a new class in mechanical and freehand drawing at Northowram Mechanics' Institute in 1857 was justified as being 'useful' and 'serviceable' to the young male members including 'joiners, masons, mechanics, and designers' in their respective trades.[20] Women's education, on the other hand, was usually advocated in terms of their domestic roles, as wives and mothers. Thus Mr Barnett Blake, an agent and lecturer of the Yorkshire Union of Mechanics' Institutes, justified the teaching of the 3Rs and plain sewing to working-class women as necessary for the upbringing of children and for the general comfort of their menfolk:

> As the first lesson of instruction, whether for good or evil, are derived from the mother, it is evident that your young females should not be neglected. Upon their training depends much of the future, and indeed it has been asserted that if attention were exclusively applied to the education of the female portion of our population, all the rest would follow as a matter of course. To reading and writing, with the simple rules of arithmetic, should be added the indispensable art of plain needlework so necessary to the comfort of the working-man's household.[21]

Such ideas were not confined to the male sex within the middle classes. Fanny Hertz, a middle-class woman with a keen interest in education, who established the Bradford Ladies' Educational Association in 1868, was also a member of the committee of the Bradford Female Educational Institute. She publicized the existence of mechanics' institutes for working-class women when she read a paper on the subject at the 1859 gathering of the prestigious National Association for the Promotion of Social Science. However, although Mrs Hertz complained in her paper that women should not be educated from the viewpoint of their duties as wives, mother, mistresses and servants, she nevertheless argued that an institute education would help women factory workers to become 'suitable and worthy helpmates for the educated and intelligent working men, who are the glory of England.[22]

Fanny Hertz's views were also shared by some of the 'educated and intelligent working men' that she spoke about. Thus Rowland Detrosier, the working-class radical, assured his fellow institute members in 1829 that the condition of the industrious artisan could never be permanently improved until the daughter of the poor man was 'educated to perform with propriety and decorum the important duties of a wife and a mother'. Furthermore he asked, 'If it be essential to teach young men the principles of the arts and sciences, it is not equally essential to the comfort of man, that young women should be taught the duties of housewifery?'[23] Statements such as these reveal how women's education could be supported in terms of the advantages to men as husbands of 'competent' and 'educated' wives.

Working-class women within the institutes were thus bombarded on all sides with the basic assumptions of the dominant middle-class domestic ideology – reaffirming their 'relative', 'subordinate' and 'inferior' status. Within this bombardment, middle-class women participated in the imposition of class ideology upon their sisters in the lower social orders as well as middle-class men. But, as the statement quoted from Detrosier reveals, the struggle of working-class women to obtain an education may be interpreted not just as a class struggle but also as a gender struggle, within their own social grouping. As Elizabeth Wilson has commented, the reactionary attitude towards women held by many working-class radical men has been one of the saddest and most persistent themes in the history of socialism.[24]

By the middle of the nineteenth century, some mechanics' institutes had widened the curriculum for working-class women and such a process continued, somewhat unevenly. At Pudsey in 1852, women could study, in addition to the 3Rs, English, grammar, dictation, drawing and phonography. At Halifax in 1861 the women students were taught not just the 3Rs and sewing but also dictation, grammar, geography and history.[25] But it was especially at the two main women-only mechanics' institutes, at Huddersfield and Bradford, that working-class women might find the widest range of curricular choices. At the Huddersfield Female Institute in 1859, ten different subjects were offered – reading, writing, arithmetic, geography, history, dictation, grammar, singing, sewing and composition – although the student numbers were concentrated in the 3Rs and in geography. The Bradford Female Institute offered a similar curriculum.[26]

To what extent an institute education enabled working-class women to improve their prospects in their present employment or aid entry into new forms of paid work, is difficult to assess. But this was so for some students. A former member of the Huddersfield Female Institute, who eventually went to Homerton Teacher Training School, wrote to the secretary of the institute in 1859 in appreciation for all she had learnt there, including sewing, which was a compulsory part of training for women teachers in elementary schools:

I am glad that I was ever a member of the Female Educational

Institute; what I learnt there will be useful to me through life – every dress I have brought with me I made myself in the Institute, thanks to the Sewing Class, which I hope will continue to prosper.[27]

Similarly, a former student of the women's classes at Northowram Mechanics' Institute was appointed in December 1860 as a schoolmistress of a National school near Bristol.[28] It is highly probable, however, that for the majority of women students an institute education offered more in the way of personal and social benefits than career advancement.[29]

As the state became increasingly involved in the provision of elementary schooling for working-class girls and boys, the demand for the teaching of the 3Rs declined in the institutes. However, since working-class women had a lower literacy rate than their menfolk, they still sought and found literacy classes. Of the 114 new members at the Bradford Female Institute in 1861, for example, 43 could neither read nor write, 26 could read indifferently but could not write and 21 could read moderately well and write a little.[30] By the 1880s, however, the mechanics' institute movement was past its heyday and many surviving institutes were offering another range of courses to working-class women in addition to the standard curriculum of the 3Rs and sewing. At Manchester in 1882, for example, the Female Elementary Evening Classes, intended mainly for working-class women, included not only instruction in elementary subjects but also in book-keeping, shorthand and foreign languages.[31] Overall, although the curriculum for working-class women in the mechanics' institutes changed over the course of the century, it did not keep pace with the developments in the curriculum offered to working-class men nor did it expand into technical areas of male knowledge. In particular, advanced arithmetic and technical subjects were usually offered only to men and sewing and knitting only to women.[32]

Working-class women might also attend, jointly with male members, the lectures offered by any one institute. The lectures were of two main types – a talk given by an invited speaker and a 'manuscript' lecture, i.e. a written talk read to an audience. Many of the small mechanics' institutes in the north of England attended by working-class women were unable to organize lecture programmes; sometimes no money was available to pay a guest speaker, sometimes the audience was lacking. Even at the two main women-only institutes, lecture provision was sparse. At the

Huddersfield Female Institute, for example, we find an occasional lecture given during 1857 to 1860; thus Mrs Clara Balfour spoke on 'Thoughts on Female Education', Mr Barnett Blake on 'Common Things', Joseph Batley, vice president of the institute, on 'Preparation for Life' (this talk was read by the president of the institute), Mr Dore on 'Heavenly Bodies' (illustrated with the magic lantern), the Rev. Bruce on 'The Importance of Little Things' and John Moody on 'Topsy, or the Power of Kindness'.[33] Such a sparse programme contrasted with the wide range of themes offered in those institutes that attracted mainly a middle-class audience, as at Manchester, Plymouth, York and London.

By 1900, the mechanics' institute movement was in decline. During the second half of the nineteenth century however, the middle classes had made another major attempt to educate their social 'inferiors' through the working men's college movement.

Working men's and working women's colleges

The working men's college movement arose partly in response to widespread criticisms about the mechanics' institutes. The institutes, it was pointed out, had failed to attract large numbers of the working classes and had catered instead for lower middle-class clerks and shopkeepers. Also, the promise of classes in science had given way to 'popular lectures and amusing social activities'; furthermore, middle-class dominance on the board of directors had 'frustrated' democratic control of the institutes.[34] While such criticisms were widely voiced, working-class agitation for radical change, especially through the activities of the Chartists in the 1840s, also played a key part in the foundation of the working men's college movement.

On 10 April 1848, the final organized rally of the Chartists took place in South London. That evening, a small group of influential middle-class men met at the home of the Rev. F.D. Maurice, a professor at King's College, London, to discuss the demonstrations of that day. A solution to the conflict and turmoil so evident in society was found in Christian Socialism, a doctrine that attempted to merge the principles of Christianity with the socialist principles of co-operation. Many of the ideals of Christian Socialism, especially that of co-operation, permeated the working men's college movement. Thus there was an emphasis upon co-operation between the students, often drawn from the skilled manual classes, and the voluntary teachers, mainly drawn from the educated middle classes. Such co-operation which cut across social class differences was seen as conducive to learning and to the stability and integration of society. Consequently, the idea of 'colleges' rather than 'institutes' was favoured to convey an ideal of 'humane culture reared on a basis of democratic comradeship': education was to start with the problem of the 'social reconstruction' of society and to be grounded on a deeper and more spiritual analysis than, say, the mechanics' institute movement.[35] The new ideal in the working men's college movement was not information, but enrichment of personality through the study of the humanities.

As the name of this new movement implies, the working men's colleges, in their original conception, were both class and sex specific. The term 'working men' was interpreted as referring to working-class men. The inspiration for the most illustrious of all the colleges, the London Working Men's College, was the People's College, Sheffield, founded in 1842 by the Rev. R.S. Bayley. The People's College did in fact admit women (for the same fee as men, 9d. per week), despite the 'doubts and fears' expressed by even 'the most ardent friends of popular education'.[36] However, although the Rev. F.D. Maurice and his supporters were impressed with the Sheffield experiment, the plan submitted by Maurice, on 7 February 1854, for the proposed London College only considered admitting women (and boys) in some vague, future time:

> It was agreed that adult males (that is to say, males, at all events, not younger than 16) should be contemplated first and chiefly in our education; though it was thought very desirable that provision should in due time be made for the teaching of boys and of females.[37]

Yet again, it would appear that women were marginal to the main business of another major adult education movement. If women wanted to participate then, as in the mechanics' institutes movement, they would have to fit into a movement aimed at men, for men and centred around men's lives.

The London Working Men's College, established in 1854, eventually admitted women but the women were never given full membership and were contained in separate classes which ran for only four years, from 1856 to 1860. After the foundation of the London college, working men's colleges were established from 1855 to 1868 in Cambridge, Halifax, Sheffield, Ancoats, Wolverhampton,

Manchester, Salford, Oxford, Boston, Ely, Liverpool, Ayr, Birkenhead, Leicester and South London. Hull, Huddersfield, Edinburgh, Prestwich, Huntingdon, Ipswich and Cheltenham also had colleges – although little appears to be known about them.[38] Some of these colleges admitted women who, as in the main London college, usually formed only a small proportion of the total membership and were educated in separate rather than co-educational classes. At Salford in 1858, for example, the number of women averaged about 25 out of an average annual membership of 240.[39] However, whereas the London Working Men's College offered only daytime classes to women, from 3–4 p.m. and 4–5 p.m., for termly fees of 2s. for one day per week, 3s.6d. for two, 4s. for three and 5s. for four, the mixed sex colleges elsewhere mainly organized evening classes for a small fee of perhaps one penny per class or 3d. weekly.[40] The timing and price of the London classes would attract only those more affluent women in the labour aristocracy/ lower middle class who did not have to engage in full time paid work whereas the much cheaper evening classes organized by mixed sex colleges in various parts of the country – for example, at Halifax and Sheffield in the north, and at Leicester in the Midlands – were likely to attract working-class women.

The evening classes for working-class women usually involved the teaching of the 3Rs, plain sewing and some elementary knowledge. At Halifax, for example, a separate Women's Institute was established where the young factory women who became evening students could study writing and geography on Tuesdays, sewing on Wednesdays, and reading, dictation and arithmetic on Thursdays. The emphasis in the sewing class was upon a familiar theme, teaching 'only what is useful, vis., making and mending their own dresses, &c.'. By 1859, plain cooking, such as will 'increase the comforts of the home of the working-man, and economise his limited means' was also taught. In addition, it was also stressed that the young women were instructed in 'the art of cooking for the sick', which would teach them a lesson in charity and how to care for their own family members who became ill.[41] The senior tutor at the Halifax college made it quite clear that such a curriculum was meant to mould the students into practical, thrifty housewives who could prevent their menfolk from leading 'wasted' lives:

> Perhaps more of the dissoluteness and recklessness of living among husbands in the working class is produced by want of good

management in their wives than by any other cause. Hence, what can be more important than to teach young women neat and thrifty modes of turning everything to the best account, whether it be the print or stuff for their own dresses, or the small joint for the family dinner?[42]

Similarly, working-class women students in the separate Women's Department at the Leicester Working Men's College could study the 3Rs, cookery, needlework, dressmaking, sick nursing and singing – as well as the less familiar drilling and French.[43] And at both the Halifax and Leicester colleges, as elsewhere, men had access to a much wider range of curricula than the women. At Halifax in 1858, for example, the men could study the 3Rs, dictation, composition, parsing, algebra, geometry, English history, geography, drawing, French, chemistry and theology.[44]

The unequal treatment of women students within the mixed sex colleges aroused some controversy; in particular, the discontinuation of the women's classes at the London Working Men's College in 1860 led a number of people to support the establishment of a separate women's college. A leading voice in this campaign was Elizabeth Malleson, a middle-class woman who was an active supporter of the women's movement. She and her husband were friendly with a number of the teachers and male students at the main London college, and, on various social occasions, also met some of the students' wives. Through such contacts, Elizabeth Malleson became aware of the relative educational deprivation that such women experienced in comparison with their husbands and was stirred to organize the same kind of educational provision for the women that their menfolk enjoyed. She mobilized gifts of money, furniture, books and pictures from a number of prominent people, including John Stuart Mill, George Eliot and Harriet Martineau with the result that in October 1864 a separate Working Women's College was opened in Queen Street, London.

The separatist women's college marked a particular stage in the working men's college movement in that a new ideal was upheld for the women students – that of the *good scholar*. Unlike the ideal of the *good wife and mother*, the *good scholar* was valued for her own sake, as an independent being, rather than in relation to men and children; she was simply a women who wanted to be educated for her own self improvement:

It was decided that the college should be open to all comers, the serious desire to learn being the only guarantee of fitness for admission. We intended to set up a standard of education in its widest sense, and we believed that the pleasure of learning would be inducement enough to ensure good intellectual effort.[45]

Furthermore, in line with the diffuse humanitarian goals of the working men's college movement, Elizabeth Malleson hoped that social mixing between teachers and taught would eliminate 'small narrowing class distinctions' and that the college would develop as a 'community' where 'genuine companionship and friendship prevailed'.[46]

The curriculum of the new college included reading, writing, arithmetic, English literature, history, physiology, drawing and Latin. Perhaps more than any other subject, Latin epitomized the ideal of the *good scholar* who learnt a subject for its own sake. The Latin class began in the autumn of 1865 and was taught by Arthur J. Munby, a graduate of Trinity College, Cambridge. His seven students were mainly young women in their 20s 'probably shopgirls & the like' for whom Latin would have been of little vocational use. They sat facing their teacher, answering his questions and taking notes, 'behaving with quiet frankness; not giggling, nor yet too grave. Not one (they said) knew anything of Latin'.[47] But ideals do not always live up to reality; eight years later the Latin class was forced to close when student numbers were reduced to three.

By 1874, the number of women registered at the Working Women's College had increased to about 250; they came from occupations such as teaching, nursing, dressmaking, domestic service and a wide range of handicrafts.[48] By this time, however, the existence of the college as a separate institution was in doubt. Elizabeth Malleson had always favoured mixed rather than single sex education and when an amalgamation with the London Working Men's College failed, the only alternative seemed to be to admit men to the women's college. In 1874, the council of the women's college divided on the issue; the majority of the members supported Elizabeth Malleson and the women's college became the College for Men and Women. A minority of the council deplored the idea of mixed education and a rival women's college, the College for Working Women, was established in Fitzroy Street.

The new College for Men and Women attracted between 400 to 500 students in its early years and continued to support the broad educational aims of the original separatist women's college. Since the college was co-educational, there was no gender differentiation in the formal curriculum. What is especially significant about this unique co-educational institution is that it offered a wider range of subjects than any of the other colleges, and included subjects traditionally offered only to men, such as geometry. In 1877, for example, we find a curriculum of arithmetic, bookkeeping, botany, drawing, English, French, geometry, German, Greek, History, Latin, Literature, mathematics, painting, physical geography and writing.[49]

Despite the hopes of some that the College for Men and Women would amalgamate with the London Working Men's College, a merger did not take place. The prospect of one large co-educational college threatened the male ethos and male culture of the illustrious London Working Men's College; to integrate women into its structure would necessitate abandoning what one writer called 'our bachelor domain'.[50] Furthermore, the presence of women could also mean that they might invade the common room, generally regarded as male territory. From the point of view of the male students at the London Working Men's College, it was much 'safer' to allow women students at the co-educational institution to join in selected recreational activities, such as walks. The unique College for Men and Women, a novel venture in a society where segregation of the sexes was considered the accepted way of educating women and men, was doomed, and in 1901, 37 years after its foundation, it closed. The fate of its rival, the College for Working Women was much more secure.

The College for Working Women, following the accepted pattern of single sex education, could extend its educational provision in a way that a co-educational college would find difficult. However, separate education for women always ran the risk that it could become gender-specific, an inferior second-rate system to that offered to men. And it would appear that the College for Working Women did become ghettoized in this way since it upheld the gender-specific ideal of the *good workwoman*.

This ideal was epitomized in the writings of the main founder of the college, Frances Martin, a middle-class woman who, as we shall see in Chapter 5, had attended Bedford College, a women's college, established in 1849, which eventually became integrated into the collegiate structure of London University. Like other middle-class philanthropists before her, Frances Martin saw education for working-class women as a means of remedying previous defective education, not as a means of social mobility. Working women would still remain working women but their lives would be enriched in a particular way:

> If they learn anything from a teacher, they learn much more than he professes to teach . . . they learn to sympathise with deeds of thoughtful love, to understand the meaning of self-sacrifice . . . The College . . . seeks to promote culture, to teach habits of prudence and forethought; it gives thoughtful women an opportunity of meeting each other and forming valuable friendships, and it offers healthy and rational entertainment as a recreation to the older, and a means of guiding and forming the tastes of its younger members . . . There are now about 600 volumes in the library, and more than a hundred readers. Wholesome fiction is freely supplied.[51]

Thus the transmission of knowledge within the College for Working Women was seen as less important than the learning of certain forms of feeling and behaviour that the middle classes considered 'more appropriate' for their social 'inferiors'.

By 1879, the College for Working Women was offering elementary classes in reading, writing and dictation, and also classes in English history, grammar, geography, arithmetic, bookkeeping, French, German, Latin and precis writing – all for the fee of 1s. to 3s. per term, according to the subjects studied.[52] And as in many other instances where the education of women was segregated from the education of men, it was proposed in 1879 to introduce cookery classes. By 1880, other gender specific subjects, such as needlework and St John Ambulance lessons in sick-nursing had entered the curriculum.[53] Cooking, needlework and nursing skills could be utilized as a means of paid work as well as unpaid domestic duties within the home. On both counts, working women would be prepared for women's work, whether in the labour market or in the household.

During the 1879–1880 session, 579 women attended the college; by 1884, however, student intake had fallen to 434. An analysis of the occupations of these 434 students reveals that the college was catering mainly for those for whom it was intended, i.e. women in employment rather than leisured housewives or single women at home. Thus the total included 107 milliners, needlewomen, dress-makers, mantle-makers and tailoresses, 52 shopwomen, 37 teachers and pupil-teachers, 32 bookkeepers, clerks and law copyists, 26 domestic servants, 21 hospital nurses, superintendents and housekeepers, 16 machinists, 16 upholsterers and bed-makers,

15 blind brushmakers and chair-caners, 9 artificial-flower makers, toy makers and feather cleaners, 9 embroiderers, lace milliners etc., 9 fancy trades and stationers, 9 gilders, china painters, artists etc., 4 book-binders and compositors and 72 of 'no stated occupation', a category where nearly all the women were employed in housework or needlework in their own homes.[54]

For students such as these, the ideal of the *good workwoman* posed a number of contradictions. In particular, the emphasis upon enrichment in personal life was not an enrichment for self development – as for the male students – but an enrichment for the benefit of others. The concern with self-sacrifice, contentment with one's station in life and dependence upon personal relationships were all ranked low in a society where self-help, hard work, self-reliance and getting on were all highly valued. Although the ideal was a departure from the dominant middle-class domestic ideology that linked all women with domesticity, it nevertheless held certain advantages for the middle classes as employers of working-class women: thus *good workwomen* were those who not only did their work efficiently but also accepted rather than challenged their social position in life. Such an ideal could lower rather than raise any academic or vocational expectations the women students might have.

The personal experiences of women within the working men's college movement have rarely been recorded. Thus it is difficult to know to what extent educational programmes encouraged women to seek more advanced education and perhaps even to use their education as a means of occupational mobility. One former student of the College for Men and Women initially enrolled for classes in reading and writing and then progressed to the more advanced work in English, history, grammar and literature, arithmetic, physiology, French, and Egyptian and Greek history; another gratefully acknowledged how the unique co-educational college taught the students to 'live happier, better and more useful lives'.[55] But as in the mechanics' institute movement, women students in the working men's and working women's colleges probably found that the greatest benefits of their education related more to the personal than vocational level.

Elizabeth Rossiter, a married student in the separate women's classes at the illustrious London Working Men's College, claimed that her college education deepened her understanding of her family duties. Although geography, history and singing did not improve her cooking skills or efficiency in cleaning pots and pans, the college classes:

> made me understand the true nature of a wife's position in her family; to know that domestic work is all-important in itself but is quite subordinate to the higher duties of a woman in her house.[56]

Hannah Cullwick, a working-class woman secretly married to Arthur J. Munby, a 'gentleman' barrister and poet, was a student in the early 1870s in both the French and English literature classes at the Working Women's College. A domestic servant for thirty years, such knowledge would be of little use to her in improving her daily work of lighting and tending fires, cleaning, cooking, scrubbing and dusting. Yet Munby records in his diary the delight she experienced when she attended on Friday 22 October 1875 for the first meeting of the literature class:

> Home 10.30 to H., who had been to the Working Women's College, and had for the first time attended the English literature class. She was in high spirits, and had much to tell me about the Puritans and Charles II; and told it all in her own childlike rustic way, with all the eagerness of a schoolgirl. 'And when he said that every good poet has a high standard of virtue, I thought of *you*, Massa!'[57]

Even allowing for Munby's patronizing tone, there is no doubt that Hannah enjoyed the classes – perhaps mainly because they might give her those 'ladylike' accomplishments thought necessary for a middle-class wife. At this time in her life, she still had not acquired that 'ladylike deportment' considered necessary for continental travel – although she could speak some French and read aloud intelligently from the books in Munby's library.[58]

As I have argued elsewhere, examples such as these make it problematic for the researcher to interpret the meaning of education for those working-class women who did receive an education within the working men's college movement. At one level, it appears that the education offered was conservative, functioning primarily as a form of social control. However, for those women who actually made the effort to attend an education class on a voluntary basis after long hours of paid work as a domestic servant, factory hand, milliner, dressmaker or home worker of various kinds, such an educational experience might well have been liberating. For some it might have represented a form of 'fighting back' against the poverty of daily life, against the views of society about women's subordinate place, against the prejudices of husbands, lovers, brothers, fathers and sons; for others, it may also have led to deeper understanding of their social position.[59]

As state elementary and evening class provision expanded in the late decades of the nineteenth century, the demand for elementary education in the working men's and working women's colleges declined, and a number of the colleges faded away. The College for Working Women, however, continued to survive, parallel to and distinct from the London Working Men's College until 1966 when a merger of the two institutions took place.

Evening schools

Throughout the period 1800–1914, working-class women might also have access to evening or night schools. Such schools were often organized by the middle-classes although, as mentioned earlier, the state became increasingly involved in such provision from the 1880s and into the twentieth century. In the first half of the nineteenth century in particular, evening schools were some-times an extension, into the weekday, of an adult Sunday school, or sometimes established independently by middle-class indivi-duals, groups or organizations, keen (for a variety of motives) to educate adults in the 'lower' social orders. Some of these evening schools were aimed specifically at working-class women.

It was common at the beginning of the nineteenth century to find evening schools teaching reading separately to men and women, wherever practicable. This was so in the counties of Bucks and Berks in 1814.[60] By 1851, most of the evening schools were held in day school premises and often had connections with the two main religious societies organizing elementary day provision – the British and Foreign School Society and the much larger National Society. At Belper, near Derby, for example, a British school was open four nights a week to any of the young women working in the local mills who wanted 'to improve themselves' in reading, writing and sewing. On the sewing nights, the best readers took it in turns to read aloud an amusing book.[61] The Revised Code of 1862 speeded up the growth of evening schools since it not only allowed grants to be claimed for those pupils over twelve years of age attending in the evenings but also withdrew the restriction which prevented certificated day teachers from teaching in the evening. In rural areas in particular, where the National Society was especially influential, teachers in the day schools were expected to play a part in village life outside school hours. As Merson notes, duties such as playing the organ, helping with village concerts, training the choir, helping in Sunday school, and particularly organizing evening schools, were reckoned to be part of a teacher's responsibility to the community. In particular, such activities were expected of rural teachers until the end of the First World War.[62]

Other evening schools for working-class women might be the result of middle-class philanthropy. At Birmingham in 1847, for example, an Evening School for Women was planned, opened and conducted by middle-class women. The ladies offered to teach reading, writing, arithmetic and sewing, and to give instruction in the contents of the Bible as well as 'the other great book – the world we live in'; it was also hoped that cookery might be taught and that eventually vocal music and 'other softening and sweetening arts' might be added.[63] The first night the school opened, 36 women entered paying the admission fee of thirteen pence plus one penny for the copybook necessary for practising writing. Most of these scholars were married women yet they were described as 'Poor things', ignorant of 'household business'.[64] In the advocacy of the necessity of arithmetic, sewing and cooking for such scholars, these middle-class ladies upheld for their working-class sisters the class-specific ideal of the *good wife and mother*:

> They [the scholars] do learn arithmetic to some purpose: and they learn something else by means of it: – nothing less than that it answers better to some of them to stay at home and keep house, than to earn wages in the manufactory . . . With great satisfaction, a wife . . . now finds herself able to check . . . mistakes. When, added to this, she has become a reasonable thinker and planner, can understand her business – can make and mend, and buy and economise, and suit her ways to her means; she may easily find that it answers better, as regard mere money, to stay at home, than to work at the factory.[65]

In statements such as this, we can see how the middle classes advocated for their social 'inferiors' a specific family form – that of a wage-earning husband and an economically dependent wife and mother, at home full time. Such a family pattern, however, bore little reality to the lives of most working-class women throughout the period. The majority of working-class women knew only too well that as wives and mothers they would have to supplement the family income through undertaking paid work themselves. For working-class wives without dependents, such as small children or elderly parents, paid work outside the home was possible; for those with dependents, the choice was often restricted to part-time, poorly paid, home-based work that might be fitted around domestic duties.

Undoubtedly many other evening schools like the Birmingham Evening School for Women were established through philanthropic endeavour; undoubtedly many such institutions were also short-lived. It is, therefore, extremely difficult trying to calculate the number of evening or night schools and the number of their female scholars. The 1851 Census recorded no fewer than 1,545 evening schools for adults, with 27,829 male and 11,954 female scholars – although there is some dispute as to whether or not children are also included in these figures.[66] Although statistics for the occupations of scholars by sex are not given, it is highly likely that the 14,405 scholars in the main occupational grouping, artisans, were predominantly men; working-class women, on the other hand, were more likely to be represented in the three other main groupings – agricultural labourers (6,709), factory hands (4,148) and domestic servants (1,317). It is also probable that the 3 bonnet makers, 4 seamstresses, 17 dressmakers and 19 washerwomen recorded are women. For all these scholars, the evening school offered a basic curriculum of the 3Rs. Writing was taught in 1,410 evening schools, reading in 1,305 and arithmetic in 1,297: sewing and knitting, probably for women only, were taught in just 12 schools.[67]

Some evening schools for working-class women were specifically sewing schools, founded often in industrial areas. The Leeds Spital-fields Sewing School was especially well known and attracted 100 to 200 young women nightly, mainly mill employees or daughters and sisters of factory operatives. The aim of this school was to make the young women 'better fitted to their social duties as wives and mothers'.[68] This was to be achieved by teaching the cutting out and making up of garments in the most economical way. However, as one of the 'lady' teachers, Mrs Hyde, made clear, sewing classes could afford an opportunity for 'indirect' teaching of a broader nature.[69] Thus an effort was also made to 'raise the moral and religious tone of the scholars' by reading to them, by advice, by encouraging easy communication between teachers and taught and by telling the students 'what better educated people would do or say' in certain circumstances.[70] Mrs Hyde perceived such instruction as a 'civilising influence': presumably such sentiments also extended to the penny savings' bank attached to the school which, she hoped, would induce the young women 'to deposit those odd half-pence which would otherwise have been wasted on peppermint drops, or other trash'.[71]

Other sewing schools were established, especially during the Cotton Famine of 1861–65 when unemployment was high amongst the women factory workers in the northern cotton mills; attendance at these schools, founded by private benefactors, qualified girls and women for relief. Females attending one particular sewing school in Manchester in 1863, for example, received 8d. a day and their dinner; millhands attending sewing classes in Stockport in the same year were paid 2s. a week and worked for three days.[72] The work produced was plain garments, rather than the decorative sewing associated with middle-class women. Thus from 1862–3 the four sewing schools at Blackburn produced 3,013 chemises, 2,949 petticoats, 1,698 shirts and 829 flannel waistcoats.[73] For many middle-class commentators, such sewing schools performed a useful function in teaching working-class women those domestic skills in which they were so 'deficient'. A typical comment was that from one inspector of factories who, in 1863, stated that sewing and knitting were a proper and congenial occupation for working-class women and that it was a matter 'of the greatest gratification' to him that so many would now possess in their homes 'a greater power of increasing their domestic comforts, and of economizing their household expenses'.[74]

As the state became increasingly involved in establishing grant-aided evening schools, the number of philanthropic establishments began to decline. This was especially marked after the 1862 Revised Code which allowed pupils over 12 years of age to continue their education in evening classes. From 1870 to 1891, amendments to various Education Acts allowed elementary education not to form the main part of the evening school curriculum, and the evening schools became slowly absorbed into the developing system of technical and higher education.[75] By 1901, there were 546,405 students on the registers of evening schools in receipt of grant aid, and women were particularly concentrated in those subjects that came under 'Division V – Home Occupation and Industries', i.e. needlework, dressmaking, domestic tailoring, millinery, embroidery, lace making, domestic economy and cookery.[76] Generally, vocational training for women was much less widespread than that for men and was limited to a much narrower range of occupations, such as domestic or office work.[77]

Evening classes that offered preparation for an office job were often sought by young working-class and lower middle-class women, keen to 'get on' in the world. Ruth Slate, born in 1884 in Manor Park, East London, left school at 13 to take a job as a packer for an export druggist firm; by 1902, she had progressed to the post of clerk in the saleroom of a firm of grocers. Soon after taking up her new post, Ruth studied at evening classes, often feeling exhausted after a day's work:

> I joined evening classes soon after we came here, hoping to get on quickly so as to get another place and more money, for we are very pinched at home. My progress is dismally slow, for I am generally tired out before I get to the class, and when it is over I feel scarcely able to crawl home . . . I must struggle on somehow.[78]

Her close friend, Eva Slawson, brought up by her grandparents, was another keen participant in adult education. Thus once her grandparents were better off, Eva also attended classes in shorthand and typing which enabled her to 'move up' in the world from being a domestic servant to being a typist.

As noted earlier, around the turn of the nineteenth century, fears were expressed about the survival of the British race, the decline of the Empire and the importance of healthy mothers who would rear healthy children; education for motherhood was especially directed at working-class girls and women since the infant mortality rate was high in the 'lower' orders of society. In order to educate working-class women to become 'good' mothers, a number of voluntary societies, often with the support of the Ministry of Health, set up various centres, such as 'Schools for Mothers' and 'Babies Welcomes'.

The first School for Mothers was founded in St Pancras in 1907; by 1917 some 321 voluntary societies known to the Local Government Board were running 446 infant welfare centres (as they became known) while a further 396 centres were run by local authorities.[79] As Jane Jewis has argued, the main purpose of these institutions was to pass on to the mother information about, a sense of responsibility towards, and pride in, home and family.[80] The activities included the weighing of infants, baby shows, provident clubs and the teaching of practical childcare skills. Thus at the St Pancras school, mothers were taught by middle-class 'ladies' how to bath a baby and make a cradle out of a banana box. Although many of the classes, such as those in infant care, sewing, knitting, and cookery, were held in the afternoon, others, such as those in hygiene, ran in the evenings.[81] In 1910, however, only 130 women attended the classes although 300 babies were brought for consultations, a pattern that seems to have been repeated elsewhere.[82] Mothers in the 'lower' orders may have been more attracted to the classes offered by the Women's Co-operative Guild, seen by many as the first separatist working-class women's organization.[83]

The Women's Co-operative Guild

During the period 1800–1914, adult education was provided not only by the middle classes but also by the working classes, much of the latter provision being part of a political movement, such as Owenism, Chartism, the Co-operative Movement and the Trade Union Movement. Since such educational provision was subordinate to a much wider political aim, it tended to be sporadic and unsystematic, especially during the first half of the nineteenth century. From 1850–1914, however, such provision became more systematized. In particular, working-class women were drawn into the classes organized by the Women's Guild for the Spread of Co-operation, formally established in 1883, at the Edinburgh Congress of the Co-operative Union, and later called the Women's Co-operative Guild.

Although many of the individuals shaping the Guild were members of established co-operative families and had powerful roles within the co-operative movement itself,[84] in the Guild's early years in particular, a number of upper- and middle-class women held influential positions. Mrs Alice Acland, the daughter of a minister and the wife of an Oxford don, was the first General Secretary, a position then held from 1889–1921 by Margaret Llewelyn Davies who had experienced an unusually high standard of education for even an upper-middle class woman of her time since she had attended both Queen's College, London, and Girton College, Cambridge University. The majority of Guildswomen, on the other hand, were working-class women, full time wives and mothers:

The members who form the Guild, are almost entirely married women belonging to the artisan class . . . We find husbands of Guild members among weavers, mechanics of every kind, miners, railway men, Co-operative employees, dock labourers, country labourers, bricksetters, printers, joiners; and every sort of miscellaneous trades-man and worker is included – cement and quarry workers, ware-housemen, draymen not omitting chimney sweeps, gardeners, painters, van-drivers, coachmen . . .

As regards the Guild women themselves, a certain proportion, especially in Lancashire, work in the mills, while others go out to nurse, wash, clean, and some are teachers and dressmakers. But for the greatest number, their homes are their workshops.[85]

In the early years of the Guild, educational activities revolved around domestic subjects. The annual report for 1889, for example, noted that five Guild branches had courses on dressmaking and two had courses on sick nursing – although instruction in basic skills such as reading and writing were also offered. Single lectures were given on Guilds, the industrial revolution, co-operation, and political economy as well as the more predictable domestic economy, food, clear-starching, ironing, the skin, the air we breathe and proper training for young people.[86] The ideal upheld for working-class women at this time appears to have been that of the *good Guildswoman*, a homemaker who, through her own efforts, would improve the quality of home life. In particular, the good Guildswoman was expected to express her loyalty to the co-operative movement through buying only at co-operative stores, even if the products were more expensive than elsewhere. The interest paid out to members, in the 'divi', encouraged values such as self-help and thrift, qualities considered necessary for the running of an efficient household. Mrs Layton was probably not the only Guildswoman who walked two miles to the co-op store, every time she wanted to buy a few things. Her divi accumulated to £12, only to be lost (with the exception of 1/8d) when the shop went bankrupt.[87]

Under the Secretaryship of the highly popular Margaret Llewelyn Davies, the number of women in the Guild grew from around 1,500 to 52,000.[88] For Miss Davies, the chief aim of the Guild was to educate women and to give them 'a wider life', that is to extend interest from outside the sphere of the home to broader social and political issues.[89] Under her guidance and presumably with the support of the majority of Guildswomen who were organized in democratic, self-governing branches, a new ideal of working-class femininity was upheld – that of woman as *homemaker and peaceful reformer*. This ideal reflected both the reality of Guildswomen's lives, as wives and mothers, and also an increasing self and social awareness. The double edge of 'homemaker' and 'reformer' is well reflected in the curricular provision of the 1890s. Thus for the year 1893–94, 99 branches held classes in domestic subjects while the lectures themes included women's suffrage, free education, old-age pensions, sick benefit societies and socialism.[90] With the home as the base, many Guildswomen began to engage in activities as diverse as pensions for widows, divorce law reform, the ending of half-time education for children, trade unionism for women, abolishing conscription for the Boer War, the campaign for women's suffrage and the legalization of abortion.[91] For example, Sarah Reddish, the influential president of the Bolton Women's Co-operative Guild and a former mill worker, was one of fifteen Lancashire suffragists who travelled to London in the spring of 1901 in order to present to the Lancashire members of parliament a petition with 29,359 signatures demanding the vote for women.[92]

Many Guildswomen also undertook a range of other educational activities. Some prepared and read a paper at a Guild conference. Thus at a major Festival held by the Guild in July 1892 Miss Webb read a paper on 'The Guild and store life', Mrs Vaughan Nash on 'Co-operative productions and the needs of labour', Mrs Knott on 'Women and municipal life' and Miss Spooner, Secretary of the Southern Section, on 'Future Guild work'.[93] Other Guildswomen might research various topics and undertake surveys. In 1894 Mrs Ashworth of Burnley, then President of the Guild, and Sarah Reddish collected information for the Labour Department about the conditions under which the children of married women, working in the mills, were left at home.[94] Such a range of tasks enabled working-class women to find a public voice and to develop self confidence in a variety of situations. Mrs Layton, a keen Guild member, remembered with clarity how nervous she felt the first time she undertook official Guild business:

> I shall never forget the first time that I had to go from the Guild to the Management Committee to ask for some money to help on the Guild work. No one would go with me, they were all too nervous. I was nervous too, but I did not let anyone know it till I got into the Committee room and stood behind my husband's chair. Then he knew it, for I nearly shook him off his chair.[95]

Through the work of the Guild, however, Mrs Layton learnt to overcome her shyness. 'From a shy, nervous woman', she pointed out, 'the Guild made me a fighter. I was always willing to go on a Deputation if there was a wrong to be righted, or for any good cause, local or national'.[96] Like many other working-class women, Mrs Layton drew strength from the common interests of Guilds-women as members of a movement.

Guild activities could, of course, make heavy demands on its members. But since most Guildswomen were wives and mothers at home, such duties were often a welcome departure from the demands of domesticity. One Guildswoman spoke of the joys brought by the double shift of home and Guild work:

> It is rather a puzzle to myself when I look back, how I managed to make all my public duties fit in with my home duties. In the first place I have had a splendid constitution, and the busy life seems to have suited me. Most of my lectures and addresses have been thought out when my hands have been busy in household duties – in the wash-tub, when baking (and by the way I have never bought a week's baking during my married life of over twenty-one years), or doing out my rooms. Somehow the time passes more quickly, and I have not felt the work so hard when my mind has been filled with other things.[97]

Guild work also helped working-class women learn how to organise a meeting in a democratic manner. Mrs Wrigley, whose husband was a plate layer, sat on many committees and then became president of a local branch. 'I can't say that I have read many books as I have had no time', she commented. 'What I have read has been Guild and Co-operative literature and newspapers'.[98] But what she did learn were the principles of co-operation and self-government.

The development of self and social awareness was not won without a feminist struggle though, at both the organizational and familial levels. At the organizational level, there was the thorny question of equality of membership for women within the co-operative movement. Some societies allowed only one person in a family to be a member and this was usually the husband. A few societies also excluded women while others demanded a husband's permission for his wife's membership.[99] Such patriarchal structures had to be fought against. Thus Guildswomen pressed for an open membership, a fight which they won.

The gender struggle on the more personal, individual level, within the home and family, was probably the more difficult struggled encountered. As mentioned in Chapter 1, during the second half of the nineteenth century, a number of sections within the working classes came to adopt a domestic ideology and to accept that woman's primary place was within the home. In particular, the predominantly male trade-union movement came increasingly to reiterate the notion of separate spheres for men and women. Many men within the co-operative movement echoed these views. George Jacob Holyoake, a prominent co-operator, claimed that a law should be passed deeming any young woman ineligible for marriage unless she possessed a certificate for having cooked a mutton chop to the satisfaction of the clergymen of the parish! Another male co-operator is reported as saying, 'My wife? What does she want with meetings? Let her stay at home and wash my moleskin trousers!'.[100] A member of the Women's Co-operative Guild put the matter in a nutshell when she wrote to the 'Women's Corner' of the March 1885 issue of the *Co-operative News*:

> The men must leave home for work, but after working hours they can attend all sorts of social and political meetings; but if the women wish for a little social intercourse, we are sometimes told we 'had better attend to our home affairs and keep the stockings mended'.[101]

Miss Davies believed that such views were more commonly expressed in the North of England; in the South, she commented, Guildswomen were more easily and quickly accepted.[102]

Guild activities enabled many women members to challenge such views and to question any 'inferior' role a wife might be expected to play. Mrs Layton asserted that her Guild education made her understand more about the law and thus when she had saved enough money for a house deposit, she put the mortgage in her own rather than her husband's name. This caused 'a little friction'; her husband claimed that 'it did not look respectful for a woman's name to be put on the deeds when she had a husband alive . . . The Guild, he said, was making women think too much of themselves'.[103] Another Guildswoman who formerly held the view that there was no need for her to vote since her husband could manage her politics changed her mind when she heard the issue debated at a Guild meeting.[104] Such statements vividly illustrate the advantages for working-class women of seeking education in a democratically organized women's section of a wider political movement. The developing sense of individuality, autonomy and power that many Guildswomen experienced contrasts sharply with that rhetoric so commonly aimed at working-class women in earlier forms of adult education – namely that they should be educated for the benefit of their husbands and children, to be good wives and mothers.

References

1 Rowntree and Binns (1903), p. 10.
2 Hudson (1851), p. 3.
3 Pole (1816), p. 8.
4 Hudson (1851), p. 5, p. 12.
5 Pole (1813), p. 12.
6 A report of the adult schools quoted in Hudson (1851), p. 14.
7 Pole (1816), p. 29.
8 Kelly (1957), p. 260.
9 Ibid., p. 260, pp. 204–5.
10 Duppa (1839), p. 12.
11 A letter to the editor of the *Mechanics' Magazine*, 12 June 1830, pp. 250–51.
12 Kelly (1957), p. 230.
13 Tylecote (1957), p. 265; Purvis (1989), p. 107.
14 Yorkshire Union of Mechanics' Institute, *Report 1847*, pp. 13–14.
15 Hertz (1859), p. 352.
16 Yorkshire Union of Mechanics' Institutes, *Report 1862*, p. 83.
17 Ibid., Tabular view.
18 Yorkshire Union of Mechanics' Institutes, *Report 1846*, p. 36 and *Report 1847*, p. 43.
19 Yorkshire Union of Mechanics' Institutes, *Report 1857*, pp. 93–4.
20 Ibid., p. 102.
21 Yorkshire Union of Mechanics' Institutes, *Report 1859*, p. 21.
22 Hertz (1859), p. 354.
23 Detroiser (1829), pp. 11–12.
24 Wilson (1977), p. 26.
25 Yorkshire Union of Mechanics' Institutes, *Report 1852*, p. 76; Yorkshire Union of Mechanics' Institutes, *Report 1861*, p. 78.
26 Yorkshire Union of Mechanics' Institutes, *Report 1859*, p. 93; Yorkshire Union of Mechanics' Institutes, *Report 1862*, p. 83.
27 Yorkshire Union of Mechanics' Institutes, *Report 1859*, p. 93.
28 Yorkshire Union of Mechanics' Institutes, *Report 1861*, p. 104.
29 Purvis (1989), p. 227.

30 Yorkshire Union of Mechanics' Institutes, *Report 1862*, p. 83.
31 Manchester Mechanics' Institution, *Report 1882*, p. 27.
32 Purvis (1989), p. 145.
33 Ibid., p. 152.
34 Harrison (1954), p. xvi.
35 Dobbs (1919), pp. 183–4.
36 Rowbotham (1859), p. 71.
37 Quoted in Furnivall (1860), p. 146.
38 Purvis (1989), p. 162.
39 Cowan (1968), p. 203.
40 Purvis (1989), pp. 180–81.
41 Yorkshire Union of Mechanics' Institutes, *Report 1859*, p. 84.
42 [Communicated by the Senior Tutor], 1859, p. 160.
43 Purvis (1989), p. 200.
44 Yorkshire Union of Mechanics' Institutes, *Report 1858*, p. 83.
45 Malleson (1926), p. 61.
46 Ibid., p. 60.
47 Hudson (1972), p. 211.
48 Malleson (1926), p. 63.
49 *Journal of the Women's Education Union* 15 June 1877, p. 96.
50 *The Working Men's College Journal* December 1900, p. 313.
51 Martin (1879), p. 485.
52 *Journal of the Women's Education Union*, 15 June 1879, p. 95.
53 Martin (1879), p. 487; *The Englishwoman's Review* 15 November 1880, p. 514.
54 *The Englishwoman's Review* 15 January 1884, pp. 38–9; Martin (1879), p. 487.
55 Quoted in Malleson (1926), pp. 67–9.
56 Rossiter (1859), p. 154.
57 Hudson (1972), p. 380.
58 Ibid., p. 379.
59 Purvis (1989), pp. 227–9.
60 Goddard (1816).
61 British and Foreign School Society, *Report 1819*, p. 91.
62 Merson (1979), p. 34.
63 'The new school for wives' (1852), p. 85.
64 Ibid., pp. 85–6.
65 Ibid., p. 88.
66 *Census of Great Britain, 1851: Education Section, Evening Schools for Adults*, pp. 80–81; Kelly (1962), pp. 153–4.
67 *Census of Great Britain, 1851*, ibid, p. 81.
68 Hole (1860), p. 48.
69 Hyde (1862), p. 26.
70 Hole (1860), p. 49.

71 Hyde (1862), p. 51, p. 59.
72 Barlee (1863), p. 87, p. 25.
73 Hewitt (1958), p. 80.
74 *PP 1864 Vol. XXII*, Reports of the Inspectors of Factories for the Half Term ending 31st October 1863, p. 68.
75 Sadler (1908), pp. 52–71.
76 Ibid., p. 108; Percy (1970), p. 150.
77 See Blunden (1984).
78 Thompson (1987), p. 111.
79 Lewis (1980), p. 96.
80 Ibid., p. 97.
81 Bunting *et al.* (1907), p. 48, pp. 58–60.
82 Lewis (1980), p. 97.
83 Gaffin (1977), p. 114.
84 Black (1989), p. 113.
85 Davies (1904), p. 148.
86 Webb (1927), pp. 53–4.
87 Layton (1931), p. 38.
88 Blaszak (1986), p. 78; Dallas (1978).
89 Davies (1904), p. 73.
90 Webb (1927), pp. 55–6.
91 Webb (1927), p. 100, p. 107, pp. 98–9; Banks (1981), p. 192; Hannam (1989), p. 84.
92 Liddington (1984), p. 104.
93 Davies (1904), p. 33.
94 Webb (1927), p. 111.
95 Layton (1931), p. 41.
96 Ibid., p. 49.
97 Davies (ed.), 1931, pp. 133–4.
98 Wrigley (1931), p. 66.
99 Davies (1904), p. 98.
100 Holyoake (n.d. British Library Stamp 1867), p. 37; quoted in Nash (1907), p. 76.
101 Quoted in Webb (1927), p. 69.
102 Quoted in Gaffin and Thoms (1983), p. 6.
103 Layton (1931), p. 48.
104 Davies (ed), 1931, pp. 132–3.

CHAPTER 4

Education and Middle-class Girls

From 1800–1914, the education of middle-class girls was usually carefully segregated from the schooling of working-class girls and seen as 'superior' and 'prestigious' in comparison with the options available to the 'lower orders' of society. Middle-class girls were not expected, unlike their working-class sisters, to engage in paid work of any kind, although it was assumed that they would also one day become economically dependent future wives and mothers. Consequently, for most of the period under study, the content of education for middle-class girls tended to stress ornamental knowledge that might attract and impress a suitor. As Maria Grey complained in a paper read before the Society of Arts on 31st May 1871:

> What they [women] are educated for is to come up to a certain conventional standard accepted in the class to which they belong, to adorn (if they can) the best parlour or the drawing-room, as it may be, to gratify a mother's vanity, to amuse a father's leisure hours, above all, to get married.[1]

It was this emphasis upon the social priorities of a girl's education that many middle-class women objected to, and from the 1840s a movement began to reform the education of middle-class girls and to establish academic schools. The aim of this chapter is to discuss both the 'traditional' forms of schooling as well as the new academic ventures.

Traditional forms of schooling

Home education

Throughout the Victorian and Edwardian eras, middle-class girls were taught mainly at home and/or a small private school managed by middle-class ladies. When young, middle-class boys might share a home education with their sisters, but once the boys were old enough, they were sent away to a public boarding school where, it was hoped, their character would be moulded in accordance with those values and forms of behaviour that constituted the public school 'ideal'. This included an emphasis upon discipline, academic excellence (especially in classics), training for leadership and the spirit of fair play in athletics.[2]

This gender differentiation in the forms of education for middle-class girls and boys was justified in terms of the different futures expected of women and men. While middle-class boys should be prepared for the professional and public world, their sisters should be educated for a home life. As the influential writer Elizabeth Sewell said in 1865:

> The aim of education is to fit children for the position in life which they are thereafter to occupy. Boys are to be sent out into the world to buffet with its temptations, to mingle with bad and good, to govern and direct. The school is the type of the life they are hereafter to lead. Girls are to dwell in quiet homes, amongst a few friends; to exercise a noiseless influence, to be submissive and retiring. There is no connection between the bustling mill-wheel life of a large school and that for which they are supposed to be preparing. This alone is a sufficient reason for supposing, even on a cursory glance, that to educate girls in crowds is to educate them wrongly.[3]

Others, such as James Davies, echoed in 1869 the popular view that home was the school intended by 'nature' for girls – 'The parents and the governess are the proper superintendents and teachers, the sisters the proper schoolfellows'.[4] Above all else, the aim of home education for the middle-class girl was to make her into that genteel being, a 'lady' who would not work for her living but one day in the future become a *ladylike wife and mother*.

The quality of home education was variable, especially in the early and mid-Victorian periods when the majority of middle-class girls were taught by amateurs, such as mothers, fathers, older sisters or family friends.[5] As Davidoff and Hall explain, girls were expected 'to make do' with the teaching of unpaid kin and friends since, unlike their brothers, their education was not expected to yield any economic return.[6]

One such middle-class girl who had to 'make do' was Emily Davies, born in 1830, whose father was a clergyman. When she was nine years old Emily went for a few months to a small day school for girls and later she and her older sister, Jane, had lessons in music and also in French and Italian from a French master. Otherwise Emily was mainly taught by her mother and Jane. She learnt a little Latin for pleasure, simply because her brothers were studying it, and also wrote with one brother, William, 'bits of English composition, once a week, looked over by my father'. Emily regretfully remembered that, as was typical of clergymen's daughters at that time, they 'get on as they can'.[7] Even novels and all light literature were forbidden – on the grounds that they would tempt young people to look on the pleasurable side of life as a state to be coveted.[8]

The education of Emily's brothers, however, proceeded along expected lines. One of her father's curates took pupils, among whom were the three Davies boys. Llewelyn, when sixteen, went in 1842 to school at Repton, and in 1844 to Trinity College, Cambridge. William followed him to Repton and university. Henry went to school at Rugby, and was then articled to a solicitor in Doncaster.[9] Emily's lack of the systematic schooling her brothers enjoyed was undoubtedly the mainspring that fuelled her resolve in later life to reform the education of middle-class girls and women.

The education of girls in wealthy families followed a different pattern since there would be a nursery for the very young children and a schoolroom where more formal education began. A girl would be taught 'accomplishments' such as singing, languages and drawing by a resident or visiting governess and possibly other subjects, such as the classics, arithmetic or science, by a visiting tutor hired on a daily or hourly basis. Sometimes too, parents were involved in their daughter's education. Lady Charlotte, born in 1812, daughter of the Ninth Earl of Lindsey, was taught music, singing, languages and etching on copper plate by governesses and, when in London for the season, had dancing lessons and instruction from an Italian tutor to whom she afterwards sent packages of her work. In the autumn of 1826 she was learning geography, arithmetic and Latin with a tutor at home.[10] Florence Nightingale, born in 1820 to rich parents, was taught music and drawing by a governess, and Greek, Latin, German, French, Italian, history and philosophy by her father.[11]

Gorham asserts that only a limited number of households, namely those in the upper class and upper-middle class, ever employed governesses; meagre as her salary could be, even £30 per annum would have been a prohibitive outlay for lower-middle and middle-class families.[12] However, by the 1860s, industrialization had brought increasing wealth to many professional, merchant and manufacturing families who, seeking to move up the social scale, or finding local schools for their daughters inadequate, employed a governess; after all, even though the governess was often poorly educated, she was usually from a 'genteel' background, a 'distressed' gentlewoman who, through unfortunate circumstances, was obliged to engage in that unladylike activity – earning a living.[13] James Bryce, in his evidence to the Schools Inquiry Commission of 1867–8 suggested that daughters in professional and merchant families in Lancashire were usually taught at home by a nursery or visiting governess until they were about ten years old – a pattern he believed was nationwide in these occupational groupings.[14] Indeed, one can find many examples to support his claim.

Jane Harrison, born in 1850, whose father was a timber merchant in Hull, had a rapid succession of governesses who, she recalled, 'taught me deportment, how to come into a room, how to get into a carriage, also that "little girls should be seen and not heard", and that I was there (in the schoolroom) "to learn, and not to ask questions".'[15] Every day she also spent time doing 'exquisite' hems and seams and learning three verses of the Bible. Her favourite governess was 'a woman of real intelligence, ignorant but willing and eager to learn anything and everything I wanted'; together they attempted German, Latin, the Greek Testament and a little Hebrew.[16] Katherine Chorley, born in 1897, whose father was the director of a big engineering firm in Manchester, was educated by a nursery governess and then, when eight years old, by an Italian governess, Miss Margharetti, who was soon replaced by a Frenchwoman, Mademoiselle Dupuy. 'Mademoiselle taught me everything', wrote Katherine, 'except mathematics and English poetry which father supervised and scripture which I learned from mother. She was very strict and kept a mark book which I had to show to my parents every evening'. Despite the strictness of the regime, which lasted six years, Katherine felt she could never sufficiently say 'thank you' for the mental, moral and physical discipline she learnt.[17]

It was probably, however, especially in Quaker and Unitarian households that the standard of home education for middle-class girls was at its highest. As Strachey noted, if you were born a Buxton, a Gurney, a Fry, a Wedgwood, a Bright, a Fox, a Barclay or a Darwin it was not such a very great misfortune to be born a woman since you would be allowed and expected to be educated and intelligent – although even in these families you would not share in the main work of your husbands or brothers.[18] Isabella Ford, born in 1855 to upper-middle class Quaker parents in Leeds, had a broadly based home education which included not only fluency in French and German and the playing of musical instruments to a professional standard but also the reading of social and political texts. As her biographer notes, education in the Ford household was not just a matter of formal lessons; there were also informal discussions of political and social events, such as prison reform, the abolition of slavery and the protection of wildlife, which helped to shape the children's ideas.[19]

As these accounts indicate, the quality of home education was variable since it was not standardized. Neither was there a common standard in the many girls' private schools that might supplement a home education. Since these private schools do not fall into neat groupings, any attempt to classify them is somewhat arbitrary. However, Pedersen suggests that at one extreme we may identify the costly fashionable boarding schools, and at the other, local day schools; in between were a range of institutions which most often combined boarding and day attendance.[20] All of these establishments sought, in varying degrees, to teach their pupils those accomplishments thought appropriate for a 'lady', an ideal that found its fullest expression in the fashionable boarding school.

Fashionable boarding schools

Costly fashionable boarding schools, exclusive to daughters in the upper class and rich middle class, were mainly to be found in London and in certain resorts, such as Brighton, Clifton and Bath. The Assistant Commissioner for Devon and Somerset for the Schools Inquiry Commission of 1867–8 estimated that the average fees at a 'first class' school at Clifton or Bath ranged from 120 to 150 guineas a year.[21] But much more could be charged. Frances

Power Cobbe, born in 1822, whose father was a country gentleman, landlord and magistrate, attended a fashionable boarding school in Brighton from 1836–38 where the bill for her two years' schooling was £1,000; the nominal tariff of about £120 per annum did not cover all the 'extras' which regularly had to be paid for. Her description of this 'finishing' school, its clientele and curricula vividly illustrates the ornamental and decorative nature of a lady's schooling.

The twenty-five or twenty-six pupils, varying in ages from nine to nineteen, were all daughters of men 'of some standing', mostly country gentlemen, members of Parliament and of the peerage; there were also several heiresses.[22] The curriculum covered deportment, drawing, callisthenics, foreign languages and English (which was given a low priority) with alternate weeks of history (where passages committed to memory had to be repeated) and geography. The pupils also attended nine lectures on science, delivered by a gentleman in a public room in Brighton. Once schooling had ended, the pupils were pronounced 'finished' and returned home. Such an education, lamented Miss Cobbe, wasted any talent since the various subjects were taught in a helter-skelter fashion and restricted to that useless knowledge suitable for a lady:

> Nobody dreamed that any one of us could in later life be more or less than an 'Ornament of Society'. That a pupil in that school should ever become an artist, or authoress, would have been looked upon by both Miss Runciman and Miss Roberts [the joint proprietors] as a deplorable dereliction . . . Everything was taught us in the inverse ratio of its true importance. At the bottom of the scale were Morals and Religion, and at the top were Music and Dancing.[23]

The aims and curricula of such fashionable boarding schools seem to have stayed remarkably stable over the period 1800–1914. In 1901, Maggie Hobhouse, who lived on an estate of two and half thousand acres with her husband, Henry, a county magistrate, sent their daughter Rachel for just two terms to an exclusive girls' school in London (followed by a year at another finishing school at Auteuil, near Paris). Rachel had been educated at home by a governess and Maggie, who did not like 'the school girl type', was hesitant about sending her to school at all. The mother made it quite clear to her daughter that she was attending school to be 'finished'. 'I hope by the way, you are putting on some polish. It is not the forte of our family. We are rough diamonds without doubt. I look to you to redeem the character of the family'. Although Rachel's education was more expensive than that of some of her cousins, she learnt, like most middle-class girls, that less was spent on her than on her brothers; thus her school fees were £126, considerably less than Arthur's at £217.50 or Stephen's university fees of £245.12[24].

As Crow observes, the education of 'young ladies' at the beginning of the twentieth century had changed little from that of their grandmothers; it was still believed that 'a good figure and quick wit would procure a woman most things, whereas the profoundest learning and broad hips would leave her in the lurch'.[25] Being in the lurch, of course, meant being without the epitome of femininity – a husband.

Small day schools and cheaper boarding schools

The majority of schools attended by middle-class girls throughout the Victorian and Edwardian eras were small, local day schools, perhaps taking up to twenty pupils. Most of the schools were modelled on family life and conducted in private households. Such arrangements were thought to be particularly suitable for those middle-class 'ladies' who ran the schools and the clientele who attended. As the Commissioners to the Schools' Inquiry Commission of 1867–8 noted, 'ladies' disliked the labour and responsibility of large schools and parents believed that smaller schools were conducted more 'like private families', were 'more like home', allowing of greater personal influence and the development and confirmation of gentle and feminine characteristics.[26]

It appears to have been common, especially amongst the urban lower middle class, for daughters to be sent to a small day school from the age of about ten to fourteen or fifteen. Bryce found this to be so amongst the 'great majority' of the lower middle class – 'the clerks, warehousemen, and shop-keepers, with the highest grade of artisans' – living in towns in Lancashire; the richer farmers and mine managers living in the country, on the other hand, mainly supported the cheap boarding schools for girls. However, a girl's attendance at day school, asserted Bryce, was interrupted 'by frequent absences' caused by such factors as bad weather or home duties, such as minding the baby.[27]

In the Lancashire day schools inspected by Bryce, where the emphasis was upon rote learning, the new pupil studied reading,

spelling, geography, English grammar, arithmetic and the history
of England. As the schoolgirl 'progressed', new horizons were
opened, including the option of 'watered down accomplishments':

> After two or three years this course is extended to include chrono-
> logy, geology, and mythology, with other branches of science and
> general information, which she learns by committing to memory the
> answers in Mangnall's Questions, or some one of the numerous
> catechisms . . . An hour or two in the afternoon is also devoted to
> needlework, plain and ornamental, the latter being especially
> precious in the eyes of farmers' wives. And if her parents are rather
> more ambitious than their neighbours she is also taught French, and
> takes lessons on the pianoforte, spending, however, far less time in
> practising than is spent by pupils in the genteel schools.[28]

The quality of the learning experience usually left much to be
desired. Bryce was of the opinion that most girls in the private
schools he observed 'carry nothing away but reading (which is
generally good), an angular and scratchy handwriting, and a very
indifferent skill with the needle'.[29] For some, the quality of day
schooling was so poor that it failed to build on already existing
knowledge. Mrs Peel, born in 1872 into a well connected but not
wealthy army family, attended a day school in Clifton when she was
twelve years old and 'soon forgot' most of what she had learnt. All
she could recollect about her school life was that two afternoons a
week the pupils 'did drawing' in the dining-room, after dinner
had been cleared away, on a table covered with American cloth.
She and her sister were not sent to the new more academic high
school for girls probably because her parents, like many others of
the time, believed that 'at High Schools girls learned to be rough'.
As Mrs Peel recollects, the faintest tinge of learning or 'Blueness' in
a girl was considered to make her so unattractive that it might
prevent her from 'receiving any invitations' to become a wife and
mother.[30]
The experience of life at the cheaper boarding schools did not
always lead to solid intellectual attainments either, even by 1914,
as Pedersen and Dyhouse have ably shown.[31] Throughout the
period, such schools were often opened by 'distressed' gentlewomen,
in their own homes, as a means of securing a living; consequently,
few of the headmistresses had academic qualifications or training
for their post. Elizabeth Missing Sewell, and her sisters Ellen and
Emma, opened a small boarding school in 1886 at Ventnor, in the

Isle of Wight, in order to supplement the family income. Elizabeth believed that girls' schools should be improved – but along old-fashioned lines that favoured a traditional curriculum.[32] Mrs Hugh Fraser, who attended the small school (the numbers were usually restricted to seven) remembered the importance attached to learning ladylike skills:

> We were taught how to write notes to our equals, invitations, acceptances; inquiries for invalids, characters of servants, letters to our elders, and letters to strangers who we were supposed not to have met; letters to tradesmen – in the rigid third person.[33]

The pupils also had to practise entering a crowded room and removing an empty teacup without rattling it. Gwen Raverat, born in 1885, whose father was a fellow at Cambridge University, was another pupil at a small private boarding school where the emphasis was 'all on Young-lady-hood, slightly tinged with Christianity (C. of E. variety)'.[34] Like many of her contemporaries she had to endure, when the school day was over, 'the distasteful duty of *kissing* five or six mistresses good night', as they stood in a row after Prayers.[35] Such a ritual was seen as a mark of the family atmosphere of the small private boarding school where the mistresses were often called 'Aunt'.

However, not all such institutions were completely devoid of any academic teaching. Gwen Raverat claimed that she learnt a great deal at her school and Catherine Chorley, a pupil in 1912 at a small boarding school in Folkestone, was offered some grounding in the more academic subjects – such as history, English, mathematics, Latin and religious studies – as well as the expected music, art, dancing and elocution. History seems to have been comparatively well taught by Miss Abbott, the headmistress, and an Oxford University Extension lecturer, although it was outside of the classroom that Miss Abbott 'could be a wonderfully infectious and persuasive teacher'. Thus the occasional afternoons spent rubbing brasses in old Kentish churches, a day visit to Canterbury Cathedral and the evening readings of the poems of Wordsworth and Browning made up, claims Catherine, for many of the 'wasted hours in class'.[36] However, since the aims of the school were to produce cultured, Christian homemakers who would preside at their 'future husbands' dinner-tables with grace and reasonable intelligence',[37] ladylike refinement was also taught. Thus Catherine experienced the painful and humiliating lesson of being told, in front of the whole school, that if she continued to speak with a Lancashire accent many doors in her future life would be closed to her.[38]

Why did the women's educational reform movement arise?

In view of the low albeit variable standard in those forms of schooling considered so far, the task facing those seeking to reform the education of the middle-class girl was enormous. The educational reform movement seems to have begun almost abruptly in the late 1840s and to have gathered momentum in the 1850s and 1860s. In 1854, the feminist Bessie Rayner Parkes published anonymously a much discussed small book *Remarks on the Education of Girls*. Education ought to aim at developing faculties, she asserted, but half the nation, on peril of their 'distinctive womanhood', are forbidden to inquire.[39] The learning allowed to women, Parkes sarcastically continued, had to be related to her so-called sphere and had consequently 'usually been contained in a little cabinet with tiny drawers'.[40]

Such public pronouncements about the lamentable state of middle-class girls' education continued to be made, with regular clarity. In September 1864, at the annual meeting of the National Association for the Promotion of Social Science, Joshua Fitch, an HMI, read a paper on the secondary instruction of girls written by Emily Davies, another tireless feminist campaigner; as Miss Davies listened to her own words being read out aloud (it was considered 'unladylike' for her to present her paper), even she wondered if her condemnation of the deplorable state of girls' education was too strong. Men overtax their own brains, she complained, and by way of compensation, have invented 'the doctrine of vicarious rest' whereby they justify wearing themselves out so long as women can be kept 'in a state of wholesome rust'.[41] The 'almost complete mental blankness' of women, she continued, meant that they had little to talk about apart from children, servants, dress and summer tours; even when *The Times* newspaper is offered to a lady, the page containing advertisements and notices of births, deaths and marriages was selected.[42]

A few months before this public condemnation, the Schools Inquiry Commission, chaired by Lord Taunton, had been set up to investigate the state of schools for middle-class boys. Miss Davies, with the help of some influential friends, successfully pressurized the commission to include girls' education within its brief. When the final report of the commission appeared in 1867–8, the official condemnation of the neglect of girls' education could not be ignored. Thus after noting the 'general indifference' of middle-class parents towards the education of their daughters, the report pointed out that the deficiencies in girls' education included:

> Want of thoroughness and foundation; want of system; slovenliness and showy superficiality; inattention to rudiments; undue time given to accomplishments, and those not taught intelligently or in any scientific manner; want of organisation.[43]

It may therefore seem obvious 'why' the women's education reform movement began. Yet, as Bryant points out, explanations of this do differ.[44] First, some historians stress that the demand for improved educational opportunities for women was part of a wider extension of democratic rights and liberty for individuals. The problem with this account is that those 'individuals' who gained legal and political rights before the middle of the nineteenth century were both middle class *and* male. The 1832 Reform Act, for example, enfranchised the £10 male householder in the boroughs. It has often been said that such action 'defined' the working class by lumping together all those unable to afford or occupy a house of at least £10 annual value. However, in addition to this class differential, throughout the nineteenth century women's legal and political rights lagged far behind those for men.

A second explanation for the emergence of the women's education reform movement suggests that industrialization, which brought increased job opportunities for women, in turn created a need for more education. Such a statement glosses over a number of important issues. Industrialization created many more jobs for women, but the women who entered the expanding workforce were mainly from the working rather than the middle classes; and it seems to have been middle-class women who were particularly active in the educational reform movement, although as we saw in the last chapter, working-class women did also seek access to certain forms of education that their menfolk enjoyed. Whether the expanding job market created many 'new' opportunities for women in a society with a well entrenched sexual division of labour is also debatable.[45] What is clear, however, is that industrialization brought increasing wealth to manufacturing families and this 'new' middle class, lacking the 'gentility' of the old middle class, sought to gain acceptance by sending their daughters to those prestigious new forms of education where the girls might become cultured ladies.[46]

A third explanation suggests that the women's education reform movement primarily arose because increasing numbers of poorly educated middle-class women had to earn their own living – either because of the precarious state of their parents' finances or because there were too few men for them to marry. However, since the education of middle-class girls stressed social priorities, there were few jobs they could enter – apart from the poorly paid, overstocked job of governessing. Improving the standard of training for governesses, and of women teachers generally, was therefore an initial key aim of the reform movement – although it was part of a much wider concern to introduce to middle-class girls a more academic education and to open higher education to middle-class women. It is this third explanation for the rise of the women's education reform movement that many writers of the new women's history, such as Delamont, Dyhouse, Vicinus and Pedersen tend to favour.[47] Apart from Pedersen, all of these authors also link their interpretations to a fourth explanation.

A fourth explanation relates the emergence of the women's education reform movement much more centrally to the wider women's movement. This focus was established by Ray Strachey in her classic 1928 book, *"The Cause", A Short History of the Women's Movement in Great Britain* and has been particularly continued by Olive Banks, Jane Rendall, Philippa Levine and myself.[48] As Levine points out, the foundation of new educational opportunities for women was one of the major areas of new feminist activity which emerged from the late 1840s. Women saw education as the key to a broad range of freedoms: as a means of training for paid employment, of alleviating the vacuity and boredom of everyday idleness and of improving their ability to fight for the extension of female opportunities in a host of other areas.[49]

Whatever explanation or group of explanations is favoured for the emergence of the women's education reform movement, one tangible result of its existence was the foundation of new types of academic school for the middle-class girl.

New academic schools for middle-class girls

The new schools that were founded did not conform to a standardized pattern; but such diversity should not overshadow the main similarity between them, namely the aim of offering a sound intellectual education to middle-class girls in an institution that was not privately owned by an individual or a family but belonged to trustees. As McCrone notes, the new schools differed from the private schools not only in regard to ownership but also in regard to funding, fees, patterns of authority, size, students' ages, residency requirements, social composition, religious affiliation, behavioural norms, curricula and activities. Most intended to prepare the daughters of business and professional families for 'more active and socially useful roles' in the public and domestic spheres. Many introduced entrance and attendance requirements and developed curricula which 'rejected polite accomplishments' in favour of academic subjects and ties with the universities. Many were overseen by largely male boards of governors, but were almost completely controlled by 'commanding headmistresses' who shared similar aspirations and legendary reputations.[50]

The new headmistresses, as pioneers of the reforms in women's education, faced many ambiguities and contradictions. As Sara Delamont points out, the success of the new schools depended upon the willingness of parents to pay the fees for their daughter's attendance and so the reforming headmistresses dare not sweep away all the old skills and forms of behaviour considered 'ladylike' – after all, few parents would want their daughters to become 'unfeminine' and, horror of horrors, 'unmarriageable'. So the pioneers fell, claims Delamont, into the snare of double conformity; they insisted that their pupils should study the academic subjects open to boys *and* adhere to rigid codes of ladylike behaviour.[51] In that way, the risk of pupils being labelled 'mannish' or 'unsexed' could be minimized.

This new form of schooling was, however, the experience of only a *minority* of middle-class girls. By the end of the nineteenth century, 70 per cent of the girls receiving secondary education in England were in the 'traditional' private schools.[52] After the 1902 Education Act the number of girls in recognized secondary grammar schools especially rose, but overall their numbers never equalled those of their brothers. By 1936 secondary schools catered for 150 boys but only 124 girls out of every 10,000 of the male and female populations, respectively.[53]

Any classification of the new academic schools for middle-class girls cannot be neat; many of the schools had their own particular ethos, often shaped by the personality of the headmistress.

However, at a general level we may identify two broad groupings –
'high' schools and public boarding schools.

High schools

Under the heading 'high' schools we may include a range of institutions of similar organization, structure and curricula. During
the last three decades of the nineteenth century, the Girls Public
Day School Company (founded in 1872) established 38 undenom-
inational high schools and the Church Schools Company (founded
in 1883) 33 Anglican high schools.[54] Endowed high schools for
girls were also founded, such as Manchester High School for
Girls, opened in 1874, largely through the efforts of the Manchester
Association for Promoting the Education of Women. Between
the early 1870s and 1900, over ninety girls' grammar schools
were established after the Endowed Schools Act of 1869 empowered
Commissioners to prise endownment from the old grammar
schools to set up such ventures.[55] Also within the category of
'high' schools we may include the 'newer' Municipal secondary girls'
schools offering advanced instruction.[56] While most of these high
schools were known as 'day' schools, some also had a department
for boarders.

The model for the high schools was the North London Collegiate
School (NLC), founded by Frances Mary Buss and her mother in
1850. The aim of the new school was to provide a sound and liberal
education, based upon religious principles, for the 'Daughters . . .
of Professional Gentlemen of limited means, Clerks in public and
private Offices, and Persons engaged in Trade and other pursuits'
for fees of £2.2s, per quarter, payable in advance.[57] Furthermore,
it was stressed that because of the influence 'of the Female Character
upon Society', it was of 'the greatest importance that the future
mothers of families' should be so educated that they were enabled
to teach their own children the truths and duties of religion and to
impart a portion of that information placed by modern education
within the reach of all.[58] A highly successful venture, the school
was Miss Buss's own property until 1872 when she handed it over
to be managed by a Trust and thus made the school a 'public' rather
than a private family concern.

When the NLC opened, the local examinations of Oxford and
Cambridge Universities were open to boys only. Believing that girls
must be assessed by the same criteria applied to boys, Miss Buss

supported the successful 1860s campaign spearheaded by Emily
Davies to open the examinations to girls. Not unexpectedly, Miss
Buss entered her pupils for the public examinations and encouraged
them to aspire to the higher education facilities that were slowly
being opened to women. By 1879, twelve old NLC students were
at Girton, a women's college associated with Cambridge University
and the following year another old student, Clara Collet, gained a
degree from London University.[59]

Miss Buss, however, did not escape the snare of double conformity to both male academic standards and ladylike behaviour.
Although she encouraged intellectual attainments, she also emphasized that traditional feminine qualities must be upheld. In many of
her weekly addresses to her pupils she extolled the virtues of the
dutiful, good daughter who contributed 'in a thousand ways to the
comforts of home' as a way of repaying her parents for the care and
money expended on her education[60]. Dutiful daughters had also to
learn that knowledge considered suitable for a 'lady'. Thus Italian,
German, music, painting and dancing were 'optional' extras, offered
in the afternoons. An old pupil who left the NLC in 1897 remembered how 'deportment' was included in the dancing classes. Pupils
were instructed in walking round the room, with hands neatly
folded in front; they were also taught how to bow when passing the
dancing mistress so that they should acquire the correct manner of
greeting acquaintances in the street.[61]

Several features of the NLC deserve special mention since they
influenced the subsequent development and shape of girls' high
schools generally. First, although the NLC was Anglican, Miss Buss
allowed parents the right of withdrawing their daughter from the
Church of England catechism or any part of the religious teaching
they objected to. As Kamm notes, this religious tolerance at a
time when Jews and Catholics still suffered certain disabilities was
brave and far-sighted.[62] At the NLC, Catholic, Jewish and Non-
Conformist girls were welcome and accepted. Secondly, since Miss
Buss believed that family life was of supreme importance for her
pupils, lessons were organized only in the mornings so that afternoons could be spent at home learning 'domestic and social virtues'
which she held to be part of a full education.[63]

Thirdly, the NLC had an efficient and carefully planned adminis-
trative structure which included a system of coherent and pro-
gressive courses, form teachers, some staff subject specialization,
systematic timetabling and, from 1880, prefects and monitors. Strict

rules were drawn up to ensure that things ran smoothly and also, it was alleged, to provide character training in self discipline. 'To be free', Miss Buss told her students, 'to be more than mere animal, one must be able to resist instinctive impulse'.[64] The rules, however, seemed endless, e.g. pupils were not allowed to come down stairs with their hand on the balustrade all the way, pupils were forbidden to get wet on the way to school, to walk more than three in a row, to drop a pencil-box, leave a book at home, hang a boot-bag by only one loop, speak or cough in class.[65] Old pupils recollected how tiresome it could all be.

Molly Hughes, a NLC pupil in the 1880s, remembered how almost every day a new rule appeared, in large sprawling home-made lettering. Netta Syrett hated not only 'the regimentation of the place' but its headmistress whom she likened to Queen Victoria. In particular, Netta never forgave Miss Buss for forbidding her delicate sister, also a pupil at the same school, to cough; some months later, the sister, who had always been afraid of her headmistress, died of tuberculosis.[66]

Fourthly, another distinctive feature of the NLC was the attempt to create a schoolgirl community with its own lifestyle, including activities such as organized games, a school magazine, various clubs and old girls' reunions. Indeed, the very first issue of the school journal *Our Magazine* expressed the aim of encouraging group solidarity and increasing 'our "espirit de corps".'[67] Many pupils did find a common experience, a feeling of being alike rather than differentiated by social distinctions. Molly Hughes had previously been a pupil at a private school where she bitterly resented the way the other girls noticed her poverty. However, at her new school she felt one immediate advantage:

> Now at the North London I sensed at once a different atmosphere.
> No one asked where you lived, how much pocket-money you had,
> or what your father was – he might be a bishop or a rat-catcher . . .
> I was told after I had left school that I had been a constant wonder
> for the length of time that one dress had lasted me, and that this had
> called forth admiration, not contempt.[68]

Finally, another feature of the NLC was its emphasis upon social service to the community. 'We want an active interest in the well being of others', Miss Buss counselled her students, a sentiment that she interpreted in a particular way. Thus in her Prize Day report in December 1850 she proposed, amongst other things, that the pupils should contribute articles of clothing, cut out, fitted, and made by themselves, to some charities in the local neighbourhood[69]. The sewing society that undertook this task, the Dorcas Society, supplied between five and six hundred articles a year. Molly Hughes' account of these lessons reveals that they were enjoyed not so much for the sewing (which had a low status within the hierarchy of schools subjects) as for the break from school routine:

> Turning her back on the frivolities of embroidery, Miss Buss encouraged both plain sewing and Christianity by ordaining a Dorcas meeting once a month. To most of us it was a treat, providing a change from the usual routine. It involved a lunch at school and staying for the afternoon, with a possible game in the gymnasium. Surprise packets were prepared by our mothers and eaten, picnic fashion, in the dining-room, rousing envy among the girls who were enduring the school lunch. Since the work was more of a good deed than a lesson, we were allowed to talk a little within reason while we sewed. The only thing we had to sign for was forgetting to bring a thimble. I generally forgot mine, but Bessie Jones could always be relied on to have brought a few spare ones, in order to meet such cases.
>
> For two hours we sewed horribly coarse cotton, of a dull biscuit colour and queer smell, with little blackish threads poking out of it here and there. It was to become in time chemises for the poor. We were not taught how to cut them out, for our mistakes would have been wasteful. Our duty was to join long stretches of stuff together . . . Where did the pleasure come in? The reward for our noble work consisted in being read aloud to by the form mistress. As she was not required to improve us, she chose some jolly book that she herself liked, and we were encouraged to discuss any little point that arose in it, even while we sewed – a delightful change from the usual procedure of a lesson.[70]

As stated earlier, the NLC was the model for the 'high' schools for girls that were established, especially those founded by the Girls' Public Day School Company (GPDSC). The Company (it became a trust in 1906) was set up by the National Union for Improving the Education of Women of all Classes, an organization that had been founded in 1871 by the feminist Maria Grey. The aim of the GPDSC was to give a 'first-class education' in 'superior day-schools' for 'girls of all classes above those provided for by the Elementary Education Act'. In order to attract those parents who could not afford the high charges of many private schools, fees were placed

as low as was compatible with the schools being self-supporting;
thus in 1898 for pupils under ten years of age, the fees were £10.10s.
a year; entering the school between ten and thirteen, or remaining
after ten, £13.10s. a year; entering after thirteen, £16.10s. a year.
By 1898 thirty-four GPDST schools had been established – at
Bath, Blackheath, Brighton, Bromley, Carlisle, Clapham (High
and Modern), Clapton, Croydon, Dover, Dulwich, Gateshead,
Highbury, Ipswich, Kensington, Liverpool, East Liverpool, Maida
Vale, Newcastle, Norwich, Nottingham, Notting Hill, Oxford,
Portsmouth, East Putney, Sheffield, Shrewsbury, South Hamp-
stead, Streatham Hill, Sutton, Sydenham, Tunbridge Wells,
Wimbledon and York.[71]

The distinctive features of the North London Collegiate discussed
earlier were adopted by the majority of the new high schools.
For example, the pattern of compulsory academic subjects, studied
only in the mornings, was common. Thus by 1884 Brighton High
School offered Latin, grammar, mathematics, chemistry, geography, art and music while at Shrewsbury by 1900 there was a
range of languages (Latin, French and German), mathematics
(including algebra, geometry and trigonometry), science (including
physiology, biology, chemistry and physics), geography, history,
English, divinity and physical education.[72] The pattern of free
afternoons in GPDSC schools persisted well into the twentieth
century. Thus it was not until 1929 that girls at Norwich High
School returned to schools for lessons on certain afternoons each
week.[73]

The adherence to ladylike behaviour was followed by the new
high schools too and involved a proliferation of rules about appropriate dress and chaperonage. When Bedford High staged the play
Scenes from the Odyssey in 1897 Miss Belcher, the headmistress,
decreed that 'no legs must be seen, nor any outline of the figure
appear through transparent draperies'. As a result, the actresses
wore the classic Athenian style of deep folds and flowing garments;
one suitor 'whose curves were not sufficiently hidden by gold braid'
had greaves constructed out of corrugated cardboard and gilt
paper.[74] At Oxford High, an article in the school magazine in 1879
warned that pupils who wore no gloves to and from school gave
'our enemies reason to say that the High School makes girls rough
and unfeminine'. At Portsmouth the attempt to control such
indiscretions included checking at the school door that each girl put
on her gloves before venturing into the street.[75] As the pioneering

headmistresses knew only too well, to cast aside all the gentility associated with being a lady was to risk the future of the school; they in particular knew how middle-class parents associated gentility with the accomplishments taught in the small private academies.

Chaperonage was especially important when male tutors entered the female environment of an all girls' school. While in many cases this might involve a mistress sitting in on a lesson, in other instances the arrangements could be more elaborate. At Bedford High, five glass cases enclosed five pianos so that each pupil could practise with the male tutors simultaneously without disturbing the other *and* be chaperoned by one mistress, sitting in a space outside correcting her pupils' work. Such a scheme, however, was doomed to failure. Sound could not get out of the glass case – nor air in. When one of the male tutors dragged his piano out of the glass cubicle and 'refused to be suffocated', the headmistress had no choice but to capitulate.[76] Overall, as Delamont has vividly illustrated, the prize for the strategy of double conformity was access to male cultural capital, those high status subjects usually only open to boys and men.[77]

The idea of charitable works and public service that Miss Buss had encouraged was similarly emphasized in the high schools.[78] At Oxford High, a Guild of Charity was formed in 1880; members had to pledge to make at least three garments for the poor each year and to assist in one of the Guild's departments – needlework, entertainments, making flowers or toys. At Worcester the Mission Working Party supported a mission in Africa, sewed the altar linen and did other embroidery for the Church.[79]

As we saw in Chapter 2, around the turn of the nineteenth century, fears were expressed about the survival of the British race, the decline of the Empire and the importance of healthy mothers who would rear healthy children. The emphasis upon wifehood and motherhood that was strongly evident in the state elementary schools for working-class girls had an effect upon *some* of the high schools but the form it took was rather different. Rather than emphasizing the practical skills of housekeeping, some of the high schools stressed the 'scientific principles' underlying domestic management. Sara Burstall, for example, headmistress of Manchester High, believed that science for women, 'especially biological science, must be the foundation of their work for the family, for hygiene, and for housecraft'[80]. And in the 1900–1901 session, the school established a housewifery course 'intended for the girls who were going home and had no intention of following a profession'. The course content covered a much wider range of subjects than those offered to working-class girls in state elementary schools – English, history, French, specialized household arithmetic, science, cookery, laundrywork, hygiene, household management and needlework.[81]

Not all of the high school headmistresses agreed with Miss Burstall. Indeed, those who were members of the Association of Head Mistresses (AHM) passed a resolution at their 1911 annual conference that 'Training in Domestic Arts should supplement and not replace the general subjects of a liberal education as given in public secondary schools for girls'. As Hunt notes, the AHM were adamant that what was important was a *general* education.[82] The point was distinctly underlined by Miss Gardiner, headmistress of Blackburn High, who warned that 'the intellectual birthright must not be sold for skill in making puddings'[83]. Generally, by 1914, domestic subjects had failed to become an integral part of girls' secondary education and were associated with the 'less able', assumed to be working-class girls in state elementary schools.[84]

The vocational value of high school education was rarely stressed. In 1892, the AHM resolved that 'if Technical Education be introduced into Girls' Schools, it should be introduced for the sake of its educational value, and in no way as a direct preparation for the pursuit of any art or trade'.[85]

Yet many of the headmistresses were aware of the link between a high school education and entry into the labour market. Miss Buss had actively encouraged her pupils to enter the Post Office (the first department of the Civil Service to open its doors to women) and this link was continued in some high schools; the fact that the Post Office examinations required proficiency in academic subjects taught in the high schools, e.g. mathematics, English, geography and a foreign language, made it easier to accommodate such vocational preparation.[86] Less able pupils, on the other hand, who might want, for example, to become typists or secretaries, would find little in the way of office skills training. In the few cases where such courses were offered, the rationale for their existence was usually expressed in terms of character rather than vocational training. At Manchester High, the shorthand and book-keeping that had been taught for some time to a few girls formed the basis in 1901 for a secretarial course that subsequently developed into a secretarial department. Although the headmistress, Sara Burstall, praised such a development she also carefully noted that 'the work of a secretarial department is rather to establish a certain habit of mind, to develop a certain character, than to teach shorthand and typing'.[87]

Girls' public boarding schools

The pioneering girls' public boarding school was Cheltenham Ladies' College, opened in 1854, as the result of the efforts of four professional men to establish a girls' schools in their own town along the lines of the Cheltenham College for Boys[88]. The founders made it quite clear that they considered a girls' future place to be the home rather than the professions; thus the new College intended to offer:

> on reasonable terms, an education based upon religious principles which, preserving the modesty and gentleness of the female character, should so far cultivate [a girl's] intellectual powers as to fit her for the discharge of those responsible duties which devolve upon her as a wife, mother, mistress and friend, the natural companion and helpmeet for men.[89]

The College was the first girls' school to be founded on the proprietary system, i.e. money was raised through the means of one hundred shares of £10 each, the possessor of each share having the right to nominate a pupil and to vote at annual and special meetings. However, the credentials of prospective parents of pupils were carefully inspected to make sure that the College remained 'select'. The nomination of a pupil was subject to the approval of the College council. Those 'not satisfactory' included the daughters of tradespeople – who were refused admittance. Although management of the College was vested in a committee elected by and out of the shareholders, the direction of the college was 'entrusted' to a Lady Principal.[90] It was with the appointment of the second Lady Principal, Miss Dorothea Beale, in 1858 that the new College rose to fame.

The subjects taught at Cheltenham at its foundation included that range common in many girls' private schools: holy scripture and liturgy, history, geography, grammar, arithmetic, French, music, drawing and needlework, with German, Italian and dancing as 'extras'[91]. Yet during the first few years of Miss Beale's principalship, the intake of pupils decreased. Ignorant prejudice, claims Kamm, accounted for many of the complaints. The very name 'College' had an intimidating sound to parents who were afraid that their girls 'would be turned into boys'. The curriculum was considered too advanced; one mother who removed her daughter complained that it was all very well for the girl to read Shakespeare, 'but don't you think it is more important for her to be able to sit down at the piano and amuse her friends?' A father who sent his daughters to another school grumbled, 'My dear lady, if my daughters were going to be bankers, it would be very well to teach arithmetic as you do, but really there is no need!'. Parents also considered the annual examination conducted by external examiners 'improper for girls'.[92]

Miss Beale, wary of such views and initially distrustful herself of girls sitting the same competitive examinations as boys, was none the less keen to offer a sound intellectual education to pupils. Eventually she came to agree with Emily Davies and Frances Mary Buss that public examinations were one of the most effective ways of exposing the poor state of education for middle-class girls and of increasing the pressure for reform. Thus in 1863, Miss Beale invited the Oxford examiners to inspect her pupils' work and from this time onwards, the College was brought into 'close connection' with every educational reform in England.[93] Pupils were entered for either Oxford or Cambridge Local Examinations, educational standards at the College were raised and the curriculum was extended to include mathematics, science, Latin and Greek. Further impetus for the senior classes at the College was given by the successful struggle of women to enter that privilege reserved for men, higher education; London University, for example, opened its degrees to women on the same terms as men in 1878. Miss Beale encouraged her able pupils to take advantage of these new opportunities and hoped, as did happen, that many would return to the classroom to improve even further the quality of schoolteaching.[94] Indeed, by the end of the nineteenth century the College itself was involved in training teachers for kindergarten, secondary and elementary schools.

One old pupil who became one of the first students at Newnham College, Cambridge and later a fellow and lecturer there was Jane Harrison who entered Cheltenham Ladies' College in 1867. After the freedom of home, this scholarly seventeen-year-old found it difficult to adapt to boarding school life. In particular, one incident was remembered by the old pupil with especial contempt. Peveril Turnbull, a young man and childhood friend, had promised to send Jane a postcard just before she sat for the London matriculation examination; however:

> No letter reached me, but one morning I was summoned before Miss Beale's throne, where she sat in state before the Lower School came into prayers. She had in front of her a post-card (post-cards had only just been invented) written in a schoolboy scrawl and signed 'Peveril'. 'That', she said, pointing a disgusted finger at the signature, 'is a boy's name'. 'Yes', I said, 'it's Peveril; he promised to write to me before the examination', and I put my hand out for the post-card. 'No, this must go to your parents', and then came a long harangue. It ended with these words which intrigued me so that I remember them, exactly: 'You are too young, and I hope too innocent, to realise the gross vulgarity of such a letter or the terrible results to which it might lead'. I was indeed, and still am, for what do you think was the offence? After his signature Peveril had written *'Give my love to the Examiners!'*.[95]

Such an account reveals not only the power of the new 'professional' headmistress – but also the way in which she might attempt to control any contact with boys that had the slightest tinge of 'impropriety'; after all, a post-card had to be delivered and might be read by an assortment of people. Other forms of impropriety included attendance at the Cheltenham College Boys' football ground and, more expectedly, the race course and polo ground – all places that were considered out of bounds as late as 1914.

In contrast, another Cheltenham Ladies' College pupil, Annabel Jackson, seems to have had a happier school life in the 1870s, despite some early problems in adapting to her new environment. When she was fifteen and a half, Annabel passed the Oxford Senior Examinations and moved up into Miss Soulsby's class. Although everything about the six foot two inches tall Miss Soulsby was 'ugly, ungainly and badly made', her class came to worship her:

> She could make us cry and she could make us laugh. I remember the whole form being in tears over the execution of Charles I and over Rossetti's 'King's Tragedy'. She drummed English literature into us willy-nilly . . . I was inclined, as all schoolgirls and especially pretty schoolgirls were, to think that nothing except social, with perhaps a few intellectual attainments thrown in, were of any particular value. Miss Soulsby rammed into my head, once and for all, that every woman should know about house-keeping, the direction of a

household, needlework, cooking, catering and enough of public affairs to be able to discuss them with her menfolk.[96]

As the above extract reveals, even the select few at Cheltenham Ladies' College were expected one day to be educated wives and mothers. However, not everything went according to plan. Miss Beale would undoubtedly have been horrified at one 'unladylike' skill Annabel claimed the schoolgirls practised in the privacy of their school houses – 'barrack-room' conversation.[97]

Just as the North London Collegiate influenced the development of the high schools, so Cheltenham Ladies' College had an impact on those girls' public boarding schools founded in the late nineteenth century – St Leonards (originally called St Andrews) which opened in 1877 in Fife, Scotland; Roedean (originally called Wimbledon House School) which opened in 1885 in Brighton; and Wycombe Abbey which opened in 1896, near London. However, the link with the leading public schools for boys was also strong and often acknowledged. The 1896 prospectus for potential shareholders in Wycombe Abbey claimed that the new school 'aims at doing for girls, with suitable modifications, what the existing great public schools do for boys'.[98]

The influence of Cheltenham on the new schools was clear in regard to clientele; thus the new girls' boarding schools continued the emphasis upon being exclusive, elite institutions for the daughters of gentlemen thereby differentiating themselves from the more socially heterogeneous high schools. Similarly, the organization of the day in the new institutions followed the Cheltenham pattern of a long morning with four one hour lessons and a short break. Afternoons, as usual, were reserved for 'extras' or for improving work that had been returned. The curriculum was similar to Cheltenham also although there were some variations. Overall, as Vicinus notes, changes in curriculum in the girls' public boarding schools remained minor until after World War I, except for adding more science and Latin, housewifery instead of embroidery and the introduction of afternoon games.[99] It is in the provision of the latter in particular that Cheltenham Ladies College and the later girls' public boarding schools differed.

Miss Beale had a legendary dislike of organized outside games, and especially of girls engaging in men's competitive sports. In 1875, she was persuaded by a member of her teaching staff, Louisa Innes Lumsden, the classics mistress, to introduce tennis,[100] and by the

1890s she had reluctantly agreed that outdoor sports should be a regular feature of College life. Although hockey and cricket were added to the curriculum, Miss Beale would not allow matches with other girls' schools since she never really lost her dislike of competition.[101]

In the new girls' boarding schools, on the other hand, competitive games such as lacrosse, cricket and hockey flourished. With their emphasis upon sport, cold baths and fresh air, these schools embraced that belief central to boys' public boarding schools – that a healthy body and healthy mind were necessary for each other. For Winifred Peck, who had found her education in a small private girls' academy repressive, the greater freedom of Wycombe Abbey life in the late 1890s and of the games in particular, was glorious:

> we had to manage to change and assemble on the lacrosse or hockey field, or on the cricket pitch in summer, by two o'clock. To many of us this was the centre, the highlight of the day, though the fields consisted at first only of a wide sweep of lawns and a large rough meadow. But as the only organised game I had known was cricket with my brothers on any pitch we could find anywhere, I was not critical. Part of the fun came from the games dress – short tunics and baggy bloomers, with tam-o-shanters which always fell off. But what freedom, what glory, to scamper about after one ball or another in sun or rain or wind as one of a team, as part of the school, on an equality, I felt, with my brothers at last.[102]

But it was St Leonards and Roedean that especially nurtured the sport ethic. As McCrone notes, St Leonards was the first girls' public boarding school to be deliberately patterned after the boys' public schools; its first headmistress, Louisa Innes Lumsden, who had been on the staff of Cheltenham Ladies' College, was determined to establish 'a veritable Eton for girls'.[103]

From the very beginning, Miss Lumsden's pupils had to take one gymnastics lesson a week and were soon encouraged to play that male sport of cricket – plus rounders, tennis, fives and goals. The link between sport and character training, a critical ideal in the boys' public schools, was embraced by Miss Lumsden as something suitable also for girls. The discipline of the playground, she informed the National Association for Social Science in 1888, was of inestimable good in teaching boys to obey and command and 'to gain patience, good temper, toleration, and the power to stand a beating good humouredly and to fight for the side and not for self. It is training of this sort that I wish to secure for girls'.[104]

When Miss Lumsden resigned her post 1882, she was succeeded by Jane Frances Dove, an old friend from Girton College, Cambridge University, and then a teacher at Cheltenham Ladies' College. Miss Dove was another sport devotee. Thus in 1888 thrice yearly competitions in gymnastics, cricket and goals were introduced between the various houses that made up the residential sections of the school – a shield being awarded to the winner. When gymnastics failed to generate enough competitive enthusiasm amongst the houses, the school magazine asked for suggestions for a replacement outdoors game. The decision fell on lacrosse; its adoption at St Leonards in 1890 made its pupils the first people in Britain to play the game. By the late 1890s, away matches in hockey and lacrosse were being played against ladies' clubs, St Andrews University and sister schools such as Wycombe Abbey and Roedean.[105]

Although Miss Lumsden later claimed that St Leonards 'led the way' in the reforms in physical education in girls' schools[106], for non-athletic pupils such as Mary Butts such changes were purgatory. Born in 1890 at Salterns, a fifty acre estate in Dorset, Mary was deeply unhappy (and unpopular) at this Scottish school. Playing games in harsh weather for their House or side, the girls learnt, she believed, loyalty, courage, endurance and hardiness.[107] Hardiness was also instilled through the common practice of not spoiling girls. Thus the house matron would not permit hungry girls, famished after two to three hours of games, to make toast, even of stale bread. In icy, Fife winters, she would also deny small 'home' comforts; thus the maids were allowed to fill the girls' hot water bottles only with lukewarm water. Even reporting sick to matron was to be avoided since, unless you were one of her favourites, you were branded a malingerer and sent back to lessons.[108]

Although the sport ethic was strong at the new girls' boarding schools, academic achievement was not ignored. At Wycombe Abbey, a few subjects were studied 'thoroughly' with a view to passing the school leaving certificate. At St Leonards, the school was 'annoyed and ashamed' when Mary Butts failed her examination for Cambridge University; she had also let her House down since it was distinguished for both games *and* sound learning.[109] At Roedean, the initial prospectus pointed out that older pupils could be prepared for entrance to Girton and Newham Colleges at Cambridge University.[110] But high academic ideals did not always live up to reality. The fourteen-year-old Margaret Postgate (later Cole) at Roedean from 1907 to 1910 found that school values came from three sources – games, the prefect system, and religion, in that order. She lamented the lack of intellectual stimulation and believed that while Roedean may not have been the stupidest school in England, it certainly ranked high[111]. Yet despite such criticisms, old Roedean pupils – including Margaret herself – became university students. What Roedean could offer was cultural capital, those forms of knowledge, ways of speaking and behaving that made access to higher education possible.

Despite such academic successes, the new headmistresses were careful to uphold, at least in theory, certain standards of ladylike behaviour. Roedean offered traditional ladylike accomplishments, such as solo singing, piano and violin playing. Miss Dove would have liked to abolish stays, but fearing that the outcry from mothers would have been too great, insisted that her girls at Wycombe Abbey still wore them (except for games) – and dressed in evening clothes for dinner. At St Leonards, the message was transmitted that the girls were to be something more than citizens and scholars, 'above all, mothers who would not fail their children by prejudice and ignorance'.[112] But such ideals were not always attained in practice. The pupils at Wycombe Abbey, believing that games and work mattered more than personal looks or dress, were 'unsophisticated, and a little awkward in general society'; furthermore, they even engaged in those unladylike activities, of whistling and swinging their arms as they walked.[113] Roedean was also accused of not polishing 'young ladies for real Society' and St Leonards of knocking out any gentility that the pupils possessed on arrival[114].

Feminist awakenings

The historians of the new women's history point out that the high schools and reformed girls' boarding schools were, in many ways, conservative institutions.[115] Although the new headmistresses rejected the idea that 'femininity' involved learning accomplishments that might attract a husband, they did argue that middle-class girls should be educated in order to be 'cultured' wives and mothers. Education as a preparation for economic independence was also only justified in those cases where, for a variety of reasons, a woman did not marry and had *of necessity* to earn a living. The idea of a married woman working outside the home was regarded with repugnance.

Yet it is also recognized that the reformed schools were also places where new ideas and forms of behaviour could be nurtured. Removed from the sheltered, protective environment of home, many of the schoolgirls had to cope on their own with the demands of boarding school life. The greater emphasis upon self discipline must have lessened home influence and aided the development of individuality and confidence. In particular, the emotional tie between mother and daughter was loosened or even broken and emotional satisfaction sometimes found through homoerotic friendships or 'raves' with other schoolgirls or staff. As Vicinus has vividly illustrated, as long as such friendships did not risk the balance between authority and self-control that characterized girls' schools, they were an important means to maturity.[116]

In addition, the usually all female teaching staff acted as important new role models to which pupils might aspire. In a society where women were considered the inferior sex and defined primarily in relation to men and children as wives and mothers, it was unusual to find middle-class 'ladies' earning a living as paid professionals. Miss Buss and Miss Beale, as competent, authoritative headmistresses, paved the way for the notion that single middle-class women *could* have successful careers.[117] Their success must have inspired many pupils to challenge the conventional belief that an unmarried daughter's place was at home. Further questioning might arise through reading those texts to which middle-class girls might gain access.

Annabel Jackson recalled how at Cheltenham Ladies' College in 1883, another pupil, Hildegarde Muspratt, smuggled in a copy of *The Story of an African Farm* by Olive Schreiner, a white, South African feminist. The book had just been published and 'the whole sky seemed aflame and many of us became violent feminists. (I was one already)'.[118] Such feminist awakenings might be further fuelled by certain schoolmistresses who were supporters of the women's movement – although such sympathies might not be directly expressed for fear of damaging a school's reputation.

Miss Dobell, the first headmistress of the County School for Girls, Pontypool, which opened in 1897, was a suffragist – as was her successor, Miss Jones. However, it was not until Miss Dobell retired that she felt free to openly take part in a Woman Suffrage procession.[119] Similarly, Miss Vivian, the first head of the girls' high school in Newport, and Miss F. Gadesden, head of Blackheath High School from 1886–1919, were both suffragists.[120] Alice Cameron, an old pupil at Blackheath, said it was rumoured that some mistresses attended suffrage meetings and one of them 'regularly left her copy of *Votes for Women* in the sixth form room'.[121] Examples like this illustrate how the new academic schools for middle-class girls could be linked to wider social and political issues of their day. In particular, it was in such institutions that schoolgirls might encounter that questioning of women's traditional place in society that was so central to the women's movement.

References

1 Grey (1871), p. 20.
2 Bamford (1975), Honey (1977).
3 Sewell (1865), Vol. 2, p. 219.
4 Davies (1869), p. 460.
5 Gorham (1982), p. 20.
6 Davidoff and Hall (1987), p. 291.
7 Quoted in Stephen (1927), p. 25.
8 Bennett (1990), p. 11.
9 Stephen (1927), p. 26.
10 Guest and John (1989), p. 1.
11 Woodham-Smith (1950), p. 11.
12 Gorham (1982), p. 20.
13 Davidoff *et al.* (1976), pp. 166–7 note that governessing, or being a 'companion', was the only respectable occupation for middle-class women because it was located in a private home and could be regarded as a pseudo-familiar position with either very little or even no cash to degrade her femininity. See also Peterson (1973).
14 Schools Inquiry Commission, *PP 1867–8, Vol. IX*, Ch. VIII, pp. 823–6.
15 Harrison, (1925), p. 22.
16 Ibid., p. 26.
17 Chorley (1950), pp. 189–190.
18 Strachey (1928), p. 44; for further discussion on the education of girls in Unitarian families see Watts 1980 and Watts 1989.
19 Hannam (1989), pp. 14–15.
20 Pedersen (1987), pp. 141–3.
21 Quoted in ibid., p. 142.
22 Cobbe (1894, third edition), Vol. 1, p. 60.

23 Ibid. pp. 63–4.
24 Caine (1986), p. 140, 144.
25 Crow (1977), p. 182.
26 Schools Inquiry Commission, *PP 1867-8, Vol. XXVIII*, Ch. VI, p. 560.
27 Extract from the Schools Inquiry Commission reprinted in Gosden (1969), p. 155.
28 Ibid. p. 155.
29 Ibid. p. 156.
30 Peel (1933), pp. 31–2.
31 Pedersen (1987), Dyhouse (1981).
32 Pedersen (1987), pp. 163–4.
33 Fraser (1911), Vol. 1, pp. 205–6.
34 Raverat (1960), p. 70.
35 Ibid. p. 74.
36 Chorley (1950), p. 210–11.
37 Ibid. 209.
38 Ibid., pp. 203–4.
39 Parkes (1854), p. 4.
40 Ibid., p. 10.
41 Davies (1864), p. 70.
42 Ibid., p. 71.
43 Schools Inquiry Commission, *PP 1867-8*, Vol. 1, pp. 548–9.
44 Bryant (1979), p. 23.
45 Lown (1990), p. 217, suggests that 'The only areas of expansion in women's employment in the nineteenth century were in occupations based on the family model and women's subordinate and servicing role within that model. Teaching, nursing and clerical work were significant additions to domestic service in this realm and ones which blurred conventional social class categories by virtue of the escape route from unpaid home-based servicing roles which they opened up to many women with middle-class fathers'.
46 Delamont (1989), Chapter 5.
47 Delamont (1989), Dyhouse (1981), Vicinus (1985) and Pedersen (1987).
48 Strachey (1928), Banks (1981), Rendall (1985), Levine (1987), Purvis (1989).
49 Levine (1987), p. 26.
50 McCrone (1988), pp. 60–1.
51 Delamont (1978a).
52 Zimmern (1898), p. 237.
53 Turner (1974), p. 177.
54 Digby (1982), p. 1.
55 Fletcher (1980), p. 171.
56 Dyhouse (1981), p. 56.

57 Prospectus of 1850 for the North London Collegiate School for Ladies, reprinted in Bryant (1900), p. 7.
58 Ibid., p. 7.
59 Anderson (1950), pp. 36–7.
60 Quoted in Gorham (1982), p. 107.
61 Quoted in Cross (1950), p. 69.
62 Kamm (1958), p. 49.
63 Anderson (1950), p. 50.
64 Toplis (ed.) 1896, p. 125.
65 Green (1900), p. 29; Hughes (1978), p. 21, p. 59.
66 Hughes (1978), p. 21: Syrett (1939), p. 22, p. 10, p. 14.
67 Quoted in Pedersen (1987), p. 307.
68 Hughes (1978), p. 40.
69 Shillito (1950), p. 139.
70 Hughes (1978), p. 44.
71 Zimmern (1898), pp. 56–7; Kamm (1971), p. 46.
72 GPDST (1972), p. 39; Bates and Wells (1962), pp. 33–6.
73 GPDST (n.d.), p. 33.
74 Westaway (1932), p. 165.
75 Quoted in Warnock (1972), p. 73; Howell (1957), p. 7.
76 Westaway (1932), p. 35.
77 Delamont (1989), pp. 80–9.
78 Hunt (1987), p. 7; Pedersen (1987) Chap. 10.
79 Stack (ed.) 1963, p. 6; James (1914), pp. 84–5.
80 Burstall (1933), p. 144.
81 Ibid., pp. 149–50.
82 Hunt (1987), p. 15.
83 Milburn (1969), p. 244.
84 Purvis (1985); Manthorpe (1986).
85 Pedersen (1987), p. 371.
86 Digby (1982), pp. 13–14.
87 Burstall (1933), p. 150; Milburn (1969), p. 254.
88 Steadman (1931), p. 6, tells us that the four men were the Rev. H. Walford Bellairs, H.M. Inspector of Schools for Gloucestershire; the Rev. W. Dobson, Principal of Cheltenham College for Boys; the Rev. H.A. Holden, Vice-Principal of the College, and Dr. S.E. Comyn.
89 Quoted in Raikes (1908), p. 87.
90 Clarke (1953), pp. 26–7.
91 Zimmern (1898), p. 31.
92 Kamm (1958), pp. 55–6.
93 Zimmern (1898), pp. 32–6.
94 See Purvis (1981c), pp. 370–1.
95 Harrison (1925), pp. 29–30.
96 Jackson (1932), pp. 150–1.

97 Ibid., p. 146.
98 Bowerman (1966), p. 79.
99 Vicinus (1985), p. 181.
100 Lumsden (1927), p. 151.
101 Kamm (1958), pp. 221–3; Steadman (1931), pp. 82–4.
102 Peck (1952), pp. 121–2.
103 McCrone (1988), p. 70.
104 Quoted in ibid., p. 71.
105 Ibid. pp. 72–3.
106 Ramsey (1927), p. 11.
107 Butts (1988), p. 184.
108 Ibid. p. 215, p. 185.
109 Peck (1952), p. 116: Butts (1988), p. 188, p. 203.
110 Quoted in Zouche (1955), p. 27.
111 Cole (1949), p. 29, p. 31.
112 Zouche (1955), p. 27; Peck (1952), p. 144; Butts (1988), p. 183.
113 Peck (1952), pp. 140–1.
114 Cole (1949), p. 27; Butts (1988), p. 184.
115 See Delamont (1978a) and (1978b), Dyhouse (1981), Vicinus (1985),
    Pedersen (1987) and Dyhouse (1987).
116 Vicinus (1985), p. 189.
117 Dyhouse (1987).
118 Jackson (1932), p. 161.
119 Quoted in Delamont (1989), p. 156.
120 Quoted in ibid., p. 156; Malim and Escreet (eds) 1927, p. 163.
121 Quoted in Dove (1988), p. 3. For a study of the early twentieth century
    campaign by the National Federation (later Union) of Women Teachers
    to gain support for women's franchise and equal pay within the
    National Union of Teachers see Owen (1988); Kean and Oram (1990).
    For a study of suffragette teachers see Kean (1990).

CHAPTER 5

'Ladylike Homemakers': Educational Provision for Middle-class Women

When middle-class girls reached adulthood, they might continue their education in a wide range of activities. However, whatever the form of education to which middle-class women had access, it was usually sharply differentiated from that offered to their own menfolk and to women in the 'lower' orders. While any classification of these forms is problematic and by no means clear cut, we may divide them into two main groups – those offering adult education and those offering higher education. While 'higher' education was associated with the universities and with full time study, 'adult' education was usually associated with a much more diverse range of lower status bodies and with part time attendance.

Adult education

Throughout the period 1800–1914, middle-class women might become part-time students or attenders in various educational programmes offered by a diverse number of bodies, such as scientific and cultural societies, Women's Institutes and Townswomen's Guilds – as well as students within the two main adult education movements aimed at working-class men, the mechanics' institute movement and the working men's college movement.

Scientific and cultural societies

Middle-class women sometimes had access to the numerous scientific and cultural societies that were established in England, especially during the first half of the nineteenth century. Some of the specialist societies were of a national character, such as the Geological Society and the Royal Astronomical Society; others were locally based. Literary and philosophical societies, for example, could be found in London and in many provincial towns such as Liverpool, Leeds, Sheffield, Hull, Bristol, Halifax, Barnsley and Rochdale.[1] The main scientific and cultural societies were founded by elite men and functioned like gentlemen's clubs; thus men decided whether women could enter, and upon what terms. While some of these societies admitted women to certain limited activities, a number also excluded them.

The Geological Society, for example, refused admission to women on the grounds that they were, at best, intelligent amateurs rather than professionals. Thomas Huxley summed up the views of many when he pronounced in 1860 that 'The Geological Society is not, to my mind, a place of education for students but a place of discussion for adepts'.[2] Huxley took the same attitude in discussions about the presence of women at the Ethnological Society of London, of which he became president in 1868. Thus women were banned from scientific meetings of the society in 1869 and invited only to those of a 'popular nature'.[3]

Larger numbers of middle-class women might be found in the numerous literary and philosophical societies where they were admitted to the lectures, usually as a companion of an elected male member. The Sheffield Literary and Philosophical Society, for example, decided at its first general meeting held on 10 January 1823 that 'ladies or young men under eighteen years of age' who were of the family of the 'proprietors' (those who were elected by ballot and had paid an entrance fee of two guineas plus an annual subscription of the same amount) could be admitted to the lectures given by the proprietors and to the public lectures given by guest speakers.[4] Thus women could attend lectures on such varied themes as literature, electricity, mechanics, hydraulic engines, steam and steam engines, optics, phrenology, poetry, hair and snuffing.[5] By 1869, 'ladies' were admitted to the monthly meetings and after this date we also hear of women giving lectures. Mary Kingsley, the celebrated explorer, spoke on 'West Africa', Mrs Basil Rose on 'Modern

Russian Music' and Miss E. Rowland on 'French Canadian Folk Songs', with vocal illustrations.[6] The range of themes of the women lecturers could also cover the women's cause. In 1871 Emily Davies, campaigning for support and money to build a women's college (Girton) at Cambridge University, spoke on 'College Education for Women' at the Nottingham Literary and Philosophical Society.[7]

The presence of middle-class women as speakers and audience was, perhaps, especially important in the annual congresses of the influential National Association for the Promotion of Social Science, a body that debated social issues of the day. In 1864, as we saw in Chapter 4, Emily Davies' paper on the necessity for improvements in the education of middle-class girls was read by Mr Fitch – since it was considered improper for a 'lady' to speak at such a public gathering. But this situation changed. At the 1879 congress, for example, papers were read by Lydia Becker, a leading Manchester suffragist, about the progress of the movement for the enfranchisement of women; by Isabella Tod, another feminist, on elected licensing boards; by Mary Tabor on the training and registration of teachers, and by Caroline A. Biggs on girls' public day schools. Women in the audience could also listen to papers on a range of other themes that would extend general knowledge. Dr Stevenson Macdam spoke on domestic water supply, Mr Estcourt on the pollution of the air, George Smith on gipsy children and roadside arabs, Dr Fletcher on the neglect of treatment in lunacy and Mr Watherston on whether railways should be private or national property – to name just a few examples.[8] Middle-class women who had access to such a lecture programme could also extend their knowledge by attending mechanics' institutes and working men's and working women's colleges.

Mechanics' institute and working men's college movements

As we saw in Chapter 3, although the target clientele of the mechanics' institutes was working-class men, women were reluctantly admitted from the 1830s onwards. Not all of these women were from the working classes; indeed, it is highly probable that the majority of women members in the large institutes at Liverpool and Manchester and at institutes in Southern England were middle class since the fees charged were usually beyond the means of working-class women. In 1851, for example, the annual membership fees at

Plymouth Mechanics' Institute were 8s. for 'Ladies' and 'Juniors' and 10s. for 'Seniors' i.e. adult males; at Ashford, 6s. for females, 8s. for youths and 13s. for males; at Woolwich, 8s. for 'Ladies and young persons' and 10s. for 'Gentlemen', and at Newport, the Isle of Wight, 5s. for 'Youths and Ladies' and 8s. for men.[9] The chance to study at a mechanics' institute, especially those that were managed and mainly used by middle-class personnel, might have been keenly sought by many middle-class women whose opportunities to enter other educational institutions were restricted. However, once within the institutes, middle-class women like their working-class sisters did not enjoy equality of membership with men – neither did they have access to the same educational programmes as the men although both sexes could attend the lecture sessions.

The idea of separate spheres for the sexes pervaded the organizational structure of class provision so any classes offered to middle-class women were usually segregated and distinct from those of their menfolk. In addition, when both middle-class and working-class women were educated within the same mechanics' institute, each was offered a carefully distinctive educational route. We can see this gender and social class differentiation clearly at work at the Manchester Mechanics' Institution.

At Manchester in 1845 a deliberate attempt was made to attract the daughters of the lower middle class – 'shop-keepers', 'respectable classes of mechanics', those who had 'risen in the world a little' and those who had been 'reduced in circumstances'.[10] The subjects studied were those considered appropriate for a 'young lady'. Thus in 1846 we find a curriculum of English (where considerable attention was given to the art of conversation), writing (which included writing bills and keeping cash accounts), geography, arithmetic, plain and fancy needlework, French literature, natural philosophy and chemistry – as well as the teaching of various accomplishments such as piano playing, drawing, speaking French and the modelling of flowers and fruit in wax and plaster.[11] In contrast, the separate commercial and scientific day school for young men that was established by the 1860s offered, as its name suggests, a vocationally relevant education. However, landscape and figure drawing, the piano, singing and dancing could also be studied, although they were not popular choices. Nevertheless, the fact that such subjects were offered indicates that 'young gentlemen' also needed socialization into social graces that would make them competent in rituals of etiquette and in courtship.[12]

The afternoon classes at Manchester for more 'mature' adult women, for a fee of 3s. per quarter, were similarly different in content from the evening classes for men. These women were probably lower middle-class wives, mothers and older daughters at home seeking a general education, although they also had access to some of the subjects taught to the more numerous 'young ladies' – e.g. English literature, music, dancing, botany, drill and drawing. By the 1880s however, some of these mature women were supplementing their general education by studying for examinations conducted by the Union of Lancashire and Cheshire Institutes. Thus in 1881, six adult women gained passes in a range of subjects that included arithmetic, history, dictation, geography and needlework. Such qualifications would help a 'necessitous' married woman to set up her own private school while the single woman might enter clerical work or elementary schoolteaching.[13] The timing of the classes and the level of the fee meant, of course, that they were likely to attract few working-class scholars. Working-class women were likely to be drawn to the 'Female Evening Classes', as they were called, established at the Manchester Mechanics' Institution from 1863.[14]

Large urban mechanics' institutes, such as that at Manchester, were also especially successful in organizing lecture programmes – which women might attend in the company of male members. At Manchester and York in 1839, women formed nearly one-fifth and one third, respectively, of the lecture audiences. At Sheffield in 1843, the lectures regularly attracted about 300 people, of whom about 100 were women.[15] Although as discussed in Chapter 3 it is often difficult to determine the social class background of the women who attended lectures, cost of entrance is a good indicator. At Manchester, for example, 'ladies' had to pay 5s. a quarter to attend the lectures and use the library or 6d. only for each lecture; such charges could probably only be met by women in the more affluent sections of society.[16]

In the early years of the mechanics' institute movement, the lectures mainly focused around scientific themes but gradually the content broadened to include the arts, history, and literary, social and musical themes. At the Chichester institute, for example, where a middle-class clientele predominated, the 1874–5 lecture and entertainment session was typical for the time. Thus female and male members could listen to lectures on such themes as William the Silent, the hero of the Netherlands; the genius and writings of Thomas Ingoldsby; curiosities of optical science; Lord Brougham, lawyer, orator and legislator; military orders of the Middle Ages; star watching, the transit of Venus in 1874; electrical science, with experiments; and Russia. The entertainments included a concert and a reading of humorous and dramatic pieces.[17]

As the organized women's movement became stronger in the 1870s demanding, amongst other things, the right to vote and the right to higher education, such themes seem to have been largely ignored within the lecture programmes – with a few notable examples. On 20 May 1870, at the request of the Stroud mechanics' institute, Lady Kate Amberley spoke in favour of suffrage for women who were householders paying rates and taxes. The talk, however, was not a success: the meeting was badly chaired by the vice president of the institute, a Tory squire, and the 'respectably dressed' audience offered hardly any applause.[18] Another pioneer suffragist, Florence Fenwick Miller, spoke on women's rights at both the Basingstoke and Chichester institutes. Thus in December 1876, she lectured at the former on 'The Woman Movement' and at the latter, during the following year, on 'Women Warriors'.[19] Her talk at Chichester was held in October, just four months after the trial of Charles and Annie Besant for publishing what was popularly considered an obscene book advocating birth control. Florence, who was single at the time, had supported the accused by writing a letter on their behalf to the newspapers. Such a brave stance may have drawn crowds to hear her speak or, alternatively, kept them away. Whatever the number of the audiences, these lectures to the primarily middle-class female and male membership at these southern institutes were likely to offer radically different messages about women's social position in society to those commonly reiterated.

Occasionally, middle-class women attending the institutes might hear famous people give a lecture or set of readings. Fanny Kemble, a celebrated actress from a noted theatrical family, gave readings from Shakespeare at the Manchester and Basingstoke institutes.[20] Charles Dickens, the novelist, was also an institute speaker. On 26 February 1844, he spoke at Liverpool Mechanics' Institution, another institute with a primarily middle-class clientele. And he had a special message for the women in his audience:

Ladies, let me venture to say to you, that you never did a wiser thing
in all your lives than when you turned your favourable regard on
such an establishment as this – for wherever the light of knowledge
is diffused, wherever the humanizing influence of the arts and
sciences extends itself, wherever there is the clearest perception of
what is beautiful, and good, and most redeeming, amid all the faults
and vices of mankind, there your character, your virtues, your
graces, your better nature, will be the best appreciated, and there the
truest homage will be paid to you . . . every ray that falls upon you
at your own firesides, from any book or thought communicated
within these walls, will raise you nearer to the angels in the eyes you
care for most.[21]

As we can see, Dickens had a familiar message for the women in
the audience – they were encouraged to seek education not for their
own self-development or as a preparation for employment but in
order to become 'better', angelic human beings who would be more
appreciated by their menfolk. Such messages might also be heard
by those middle-class women who became students within the
working men's college movement.

Within the working men's college movement, yet again, men
mainly controlled who entered, and upon what terms. However,
in contrast with the mechanics' institute movement, we find in
the working men's college movement discussion about recruiting
'working women' rather than middle-class 'ladies'.[22] Nevertheless,
the fees of some of the colleges plus the timing of the classes would
attract only those in the more affluent sections of the working
class/lower middle class and exclude poor women. At the London
Working Men's College, for example, the termly fees for the
women's day classes in 1859 were 2s. for one day per week, 3s. 6d.
for two, 4s. for three and 5s. for four; similarly, the South London
Working Men's College in Blackfriars Road charged in 1868 a flat
rate of 4s. per term for its daytime women's class.[23]

The curriculum in the separate women's classes at the London
Working Men's College, first offered from January 1856, covered
a range of subjects that could broaden general knowledge, and also
lead to the acquisition of a few ladylike accomplishments and
household skills. General knowledge might be extended by the
classes in reading, writing, arithmetic, English, geography, history,
natural history and the Bible, although it appears that the level in
some of these subjects was not high. English, for example, merely
covered the teaching of grammar and did not stretch to the essay

writing and study of literature undertaken by the male students.[24] The singing, botany and drawing classes, the latter being taught by the young Octavia Hill, later a prominent social reformer, could lead to the acquisition of 'ladylike' accomplishments. Household skills, on the other hand, might be enhanced by the lectures on household economy since they covered such topics as home-ventilation, stoves, fuel, lighting apparatus, washing, cleaning and the principles of economical cookery.[25]

The 'necessitous' single female student who could not afford to be a daughter at home may have hoped that college classes would help to prepare her for employment. By 1860, the year when the women's classes were discontinued, late afternoon classes, from 4–5 p.m., were also offered from Monday to Saturday, in writing, book-keeping, grammar, reading, history and arithmetic – all subjects that might aid entry into such jobs as sales assistant and clerical worker. Similar hopes may have been shared by those young women too old for a day school, who were attending, in the late 1860s, the afternoon classes at the South London Working Men's College in French, drawing, book-keeping, reading, grammar, arithmetic, writing from dictation, history, geography and the Bible.[26] But for the young women at both colleges, the female curriculum was far less extensive than the men's curriculum, and was clearly differentiated from it. At the London Working Men's College, for example, men were offered not only a larger number of classes, 25 in all, but also a much wider range, including algebra, geometry, mechanics, physiology, geology, chemistry, botany, drawing, Latin, Greek, French, logic, politics and the history of the working classes of England.[27]

Like the mechanics' institutes, the working men's colleges organized lecture programmes, when possible, and many of the colleges admitted women to these evening talks when they were wives and relatives of male members. The lectures tended towards literary, social and general interest themes – although scientific issues were not completely ignored. At Cambridge Working Men's College in 1859, lectures were arranged on ancient Jerusalem, the Alps, the works of Leonardo da Vinci, the history of Cambridge and chemistry or geography. At Cheltenham during 1885–6 the lecture topics included ice and its work in earth shaping, the age of reptiles, church lands, Chaucer, sculpture and its gods, and the charm of life in art. At the South London College from 1868 to 1880 the Saturday talks included the co-education of men and women, geometry and its practical application, the life of Dr Johnson, the aims of moral and mental culture, the construction of the Rosse telescope, chemical astronomy, the human hand and the study of poetry and art. The Saturday lectures at the London Working Men's College in the 1890s were frequently attended by women who could hear a range of themes that covered travel, art, and social and political issues. The lecture in 1894 on Velasquez and Rembrandt, for example, was especially attended by art students, 'a great many ladies among them'.[28]

At other times, middle-class women could hear one of their own sex and social class background giving a lecture. At Cheltenham Working Men's College, Dorothea Beale, headmistress of Cheltenham Ladies' College, spoke on 'Self support and self government from the point of view, not of the individual, but of the College'.[29] But it was especially at the London Working Men's College, from the 1890s, that we find women speakers. Many of these lecturers had been amongst the first generation of university educated women or were otherwise involved with the movement for women's higher education. In February 1891, Jane Harrison, an old pupil from Cheltenham Ladies' College and one of the first women students (1874–9) and later fellow and lecturer at Newnham College, University of Cambridge, drew a large crowd for her talk on 'The Parthenon Marbles – in special relation to recent investigations'. The same year Mrs Charlotte Green, a member of a group promoting the education of women at Oxford University, spoke on trade in a medieval town. In 1895, Millicent Garrett Fawcett, one of the leaders of the non-militant section of the women's suffrage movement, spoke on 'Ideals of womanhood, old and new'. In 1897, Miss Penrose, the Principal of Bedford College for Women, University of London, well known for her lectures on classical archaeology, also spoke at the London college. She had been the first woman to be placed in the First Class in 'Literae Humaniores' at Oxford University and was to become principal of Somerville College, Oxford. In 1898, Mrs Verall, who as Miss Merrifield was a student at Newnham College in the late 1870s, spoke on the goddesses of Athens.[30] Although it is difficult to trace the content of these lectures, many of these female lecturers would have opened up discussion about the place of women in late Victorian society.

By the end of the nineteenth century, both the mechanics' institute and working men's college movements were in decline. And middle-class women seeking adult education were likely to be drawn into the new educational forms that developed in the twentieth century – such as the Women's Institutes founded in rural areas and the Townswomen's Guilds.

Women's Institutes and Townswomen's Guilds

The first Women's Institute in Britain was established in 1915, in the Anglesey village of Llanfairpwllgwyngyllgogerychwyrndrobwllllantysiliogogogoch, famous for its long name. The next few years were a time of growth so that by the end of 1921, there were 2,580 institutes with a 160,000 membership.[31] Initially, the Women's Institutes were concerned with war activities, such as knitting and bottling fruit, although other crafts, such as weaving, lace-making, glove-making, basketwork, rug-making and toy-making were also popular. Music (especially choral music), drama and folk-dancing also soon became an integral part of an institute's programme. Indeed, after the first monthly meeting of the first institute established in Wales, the members listened to 'selections on the harp played by Miss Thomas'.[32]

The Townswomen's Guilds movement was founded to offer to town women similar activities to those organized by the Women's Institutes. Margery Corbett Ashby, one of the founders of the first guild at Haywards Heath, Sussex, in 1929, claimed that the aim of the new organizations was to give 'the ordinary woman at home' in the towns 'not only training in and enjoyment of arts and crafts but also training in the responsibility of citizenship'.[33] Citizenship for women was, of course, an especially relevant issue at this time since one year earlier, in 1928, the right of women over the age of 21 to vote on the same terms as men had finally been won. However, training for citizenship seems to have been less popular in guild activities than domestic crafts. An analysis in 1933 of the annual reports of 120 local guilds revealed that the most popular lectures or demonstrations were on such subjects as rugmaking, dressmaking, toy-making, embroidery and glovemaking; next in popularity came homecraft and gardening, then civics – with health at the bottom of the list.[34] As Mary Stott comments, nowhere was the status of women or the education of women to make good use of the vote mentioned at all.[35]

Informal self education

Although throughout the period under study middle-class women might attend some of the forms of adult education discussed so far, 'informal' self education, especially through reading, was an important activity for many. Louisa Martindale, for example, an upper middle-class widow bringing up her two daughters in Sussex, had a long interest in women's issues and during the 1880s read widely on this theme. Her reading included Mary Wollstonecraft's classic feminist text of 1792 *A Vindication of the Rights of Woman*, the *Englishwoman's Journal* (a feminist magazine that exposed, amongst other things, the obstacles to the employment of educated women), and a range of other material that told of women's struggle to gain property rights within marriage and entry into male dominated professions.[36] Such self education undoubtedly contributed to her liberal suffragette views.

Of course, not all women readers, even when the material was feminist, became converts to 'the cause'. Eliza Lynn Linton, who admired Wollstonecraft's masterpiece, nevertheless became a leading female opponent of women's rights in Victorian England. When a young woman, Eliza was an avid reader of Greek mythology and also of George Sands's novels about free love and socialism.[37] Such self education through reading plus the more formalized adult education that we have considered were not, however, the only educational forms in which middle-class women might participate. Especially important was the successful fight for women to become students in higher education.

Higher education

At the beginning of the nineteenth century, women were largely denied access to higher education and were ill prepared for it anyway by their formal schooling. The universities were 'strongholds of masculine privilege',[38] denying entrance to the female sex. There were a few isolated examples where women were granted access to certain lectures, but they were usually denied the right to follow the same course as men, to sit the same examinations and be awarded a degree. In Scotland, for example, John Anderson, Professor of Natural Philosophy at Glasgow University, who died in 1796, stipulated in his will that a rival university be established which offered, at least once a year, a 'Ladies Course of Physical Lectures'. Such a course would, he hoped, make the women the 'most accomplished Ladies in Europe' – provided, of course, that none who were 'giddy or incorrect in their manners' were admitted.[39] In England, from 1828, women could attend the men's lectures at both King's and University College, London. However, the standard of the London University colleges made them inaccessible to all but exceptionally placed or exceptionally gifted women. Furthermore, many traditionalists felt that it was too 'advanced' and 'not ladylike' for women to share the lectures with the men.[40]

Ladies' colleges

The first important attempt to provide some form of higher education for women came with the foundation of Queen's College, in 1848, in Harley Street, London. Originally conceived as an institution for raising the educational qualifications of governesses, it also admitted girls from the age of twelve and provided 'not much more than a good secondary education'.[41] Since the new college was outside the university sector and posed little threat to the male terrain of higher education, it attracted little opposition and much support from male university academics; support from the clergy and other members of the Church of England also helped to secure its success – indeed, Church of England clergymen formed a significant number of Queen's College professors. The new college even enjoyed royal patronage through the interest of Miss Murray, Maid of Honour to Queen Victoria.[42]

In 1849, another separate college for women was founded in Bedford Square by Mrs Elizabeth Reid, a wealthy Unitarian with a keen interest in women's education. Although there was no hostility on Mrs Reid's part to Queen's, it is probable that she objected to certain aspects of its organization, in particular, the absence of women on the governing body and the strong influence of the Church of England.[43] Although both colleges really provided education of only a secondary standard, both were drawn into university work after 1878 when women were finally admitted to London University degrees on the same terms as men – although Queen's, unlike Bedford, was not destined for university status.

The number of middle-class women who attended these women's colleges and in later life became involved in the women's movement or in public life is remarkable. Early students at Queen's included

Dorothea Beale and Frances Mary Buss who, as we saw in Chapter 4, both became in later life influential headmistresses of academic schools for middle-class girls; Sophia Jex Blake, a future pioneer in the medical education of women; Frances Martin, future headmistress of the school attached to Bedford College and, as we saw in Chapter 3, founder of the College for Working Women, and Jane Frances Dove, later headmistress (as mentioned in Chapter 4) of St Leonards, a girls' boarding school in Fife, Scotland.

Students at Bedford College included Anna Swanwick, Barbara Leigh Smith (later Madame Bodichon) and Dorothy Lawrence. Anna Swanwick became a learned Greek and Hebrew scholar and was one of the first women to receive an Honorary Doctor's degree – from Aberdeen University. She was an early supporter of reform in women's education and later also an advocate of women's suffrage. Barbara Bodichon became a campaigner for women's rights. In the 1850s she petitioned for changes in the Married Women's Property Acts which allowed wives no control over their own money, and in her book *Women and Work*, published in 1857, she argued forcibly for the right of women to employment. In 1858, with her close friend Bessie Rayner Parkes, she founded the *Englishwoman's Journal* which became an important forum for feminist articles and debate. Barbara was also active in the campaign for the reform of women's education and for women's suffrage. Dorothy Lawrence, together with her sisters Millicent and Penelope, became one of the founders of the most prestigious of all the girls' boarding schools, Roedean.

Most of these women found student life enthralling, even euphoric. Mary Buss in a letter to Dorothea Beale in 1889 remembered her days at Queen's in 1849 when she attended the free evening classes for governess:

> Queen's College opened a new life to me, I mean intellectually. To come into contact with the minds of such men [the lecturers] was indeed delightful, and it was a new experience to me and to most of the women who were fortunate enough to become students.[44]

Sophia Jex Blake, whose parents were evangelical Anglicans from the landed gentry, was eventually allowed by her father to become a student at Queen's from 1858 to 1861. For the spirited, tempestuous Sophia, college life was 'an elysium on earth . . . I am as happy as a queen. Work and independence. What can be more charming? Really perfection'.[45]

Although the foundation of Queen's and Bedford colleges were important steps in the movement to open higher education to women, the key struggles mobilized in the 1860s when women fought for the right to enter the universities on the same terms as men.

University education

The first major attempt to gain access to university study was through part time extension classes. University extension is said to have begun in 1867 when various associations of middle-class women invited James Stuart, a Cambridge don, to deliver a course of lectures in Liverpool, Manchester, Sheffield and Leeds. Since a number of the women concerned were teachers or governesses and wished to improve the standard of women's education generally, they asked for lectures on the theory and methods of education – a theme that Stuart felt unable to speak about, offering instead a course on the history of astronomy.[46] The women's movement therefore, and especially the North of England Council for Promoting the Higher Education of Women, was an important pressure group (although not the only one) in bringing into being part time higher education for adults who were taught in various centres outside the university walls.

The presence of so many 'ladies' within the university extension movement inevitably helped to shape its form. In particular, two features which later became a hallmark of university extension teaching – the printed syllabus and the written work – resulted directly from the fact that Stuart's early audiences were middle-class women. Thus since the standard of education of his students was poor, Stuart at his first lecture advised every student to make notes after each talk; in order to help the note-taking, he gave each student a printed syllabus of his talk. He soon found, however, that giving out the syllabus at the beginning, rather than the end, of each lecture helped the students to follow what was said. From such a practice grew the custom of the printed syllabus in university extension classes. The introduction of written work as a pedagogic device is best told in Stuart's own words:

> I had circulated early in the autumn a letter amongst those intending to attend the lectures, suggesting several suitable books to be read, and stating that an opportunity would be given after the lecture for

questions. But I found that a considerable amount of excitement prevailed on the impropriety of a number of young ladies asking questions of, or being questioned by, a young man . . . I solved the difficulty by bringing to the first lecture three or four questions in print, which I distributed with the statement that if answers were sent to me by post, two clear days before the next lecture, I would then return them, corrected. Thus all the dangers attaching to personal intercourse would be avoided . . . This was the origin of the questions which have since accompanied all University Extension lectures.[47]

These women students were obviously very keen since of the six hundred students in the various extension centres, three hundred sent Stuart written work. With great difficulty, he marked the work in time for the next lecture. The exercise was instructive, however, since he discovered where he had given insufficient detail in his lectures. 'The ladies', he summed up, 'took full advantage of their opportunities, and certainly worked very hard, and were very much interested'.[48]

Middle-class women continued to be the main stalwart of the university extension movement up to 1914; one estimate suggested that they formed two-thirds of the Oxford Extension classes in 1888–9.[49] In Nottingham, 'ladies' were particularly concentrated in the day courses where fees could be as high as a guinea for a term of twelve weeks; they also formed a large number of the evening students.[50] Edward Carpenter, an extension lecturer, also noted that his students (in Yorkshire) were of the 'young lady' class.[51] In some areas, however, the social class background was mixed, as in the political economy course in Nottingham where of the 27 women who sat the examination, seven were daughters of manufacturers, two were daughters of a minister, twelve were daughters of tradesmen and six were milliners.[52] Overall, however, the university extension movement largely by-passed working-class women.[53] The curricula offered, the levels of literacy demanded, the solidly middle-class male ethos of university life and the ritual governing interaction between an elite male lecturer and a woman of the 'lower orders' would have been forbidding to all but the most determined of working-class women. One such person was Cissy Foley, a Lancashire factory worker. Cissy studied the poetry of Robert Browning on an Oxford University extension course held at Manchester University. Her involvement in the women's movement, as a non-militant radical suffragist, led to a keen interest in social and political issues of the day. Cissy and her friends would discuss topics such as politics, men, votes for women and culture – while devouring lots of home-made, currant bread![54]

Undoubtedly many women students were uplifted by the experience of a part-time university education. The contact with male lecturers (few were women) of high academic ability, the encouragement to read, to sift and evaluate evidence, and the chance to write a well argued, coherent essay must have focused and enhanced the scholarly ambitions of many.[55] 'University extension', wrote one early woman student, 'came as a gift from heaven'.[56] Others may have been more critical, especially if their lecturers had poor teaching skills. Edward Carpenter, for example, confessed to being an 'abominably bad speaker' and taking about seven years to feel at ease in his job.[57] Such factors, of course, helped to fuel male opposition to the higher education of women. *The Saturday Review*, a conservative newspaper, protested that university extension was officered by 'boys' for the benefit of young ladies while another protagonist pointed out in 1894 that the 'pretended' extension only provided an opportunity for 'schoolgirls' and their teachers to test their knowledge.[58] Such arguments against the presence of women were not the only criticisms of the university extension scheme, though.

Key campaigners within the women's education reform movement, such as Emily Davies, became concerned that part-time university classes might become a substitute for full-time, undergraduate education for women. In particular, Miss Davies wanted women's colleges that were an integral part of university life, where the students studied the same subjects as men; local university extension lectures for women ran the risk of catering to women's needs and being second best to full time study.[59] Such a viewpoint directly challenged the dominant middle-class domestic ideology that women should ideally be wives and mothers, ladylike homemakers, creatures who were relative to men – as well as inferior and subordinate to them.

The opposition view to women's higher education was forcibly expressed in 1868 by one of their own sex, Sarah Sewell, an anti-feminist and antisuffragist writer:

> . . . profoundly educated women rarely make good wives or mothers. The pride of knowledge does not amalgamate well with the every-day matter of fact rearing of children, and women who have

stored their minds with Latin and Greek seldom have much knowledge of pies and puddings, nor do they enjoy the hard and uninteresting work of attending to the wants of little children.[60]

Other middle-class commentators warned that men would rarely choose a wife from the ranks of educated women or, as James Davies preferred to phrase it, 'ladies who have courted the appellation of 'blues' ' (i.e. blue stockings).[61] *The Saturday Review* complained that the urgent need was to prepare the female sex for their matronly role within the home rather than press for a collegiate university life for women. Women needed to be taught, it was argued, how to manage young children, rule the economy of a home, treat servants as human beings, sympathize with and supplement 'a man's mind and heart' and, above all else, win the confidence and elevate the instincts of those young women and men who were their daughters and sons.[62]

The pioneers of women's full time higher education, therefore, had to fight for a new ideal of middle-class femininity, the ideal of the *new woman* who could study the same subjects as men and enter paid, professional employment. The issue of whether women should follow the same or separate courses to men, and whether they should take the same or separate examinations was, however, a dividing factor amongst the advocates of women's education at the ancient universities of Cambridge and Oxford.

Largely due to the initiative and hard work of Emily Davies, a women's college was formally opened at Hitchin, Herts, in October 1869, with the aim of preparing female students for the entrance examinations of Cambridge University. Nearly all the early students who went to Hitchin had to encounter some opposition and disapproval from their family and friends. The thirty-year-old Anna Lloyd, the youngest and only daughter at home in a Quaker family of nine, became homeless after her parents died and the large family house was taken over by an elder brother who was soon to marry. She went travelling and amongst the many people she met in 1868 was Emily Davies who told her about the new college for women. Fired with an ambition to go to Hitchin, Anna found that her married sisters and friends were astonished when she told them of her decision. 'I see they think it would be much better if I was going to be married', she reflected. After four terms at the college, however, Anna's sisters eventually persuaded her to leave, accusing her of self-indulgence. The once aspiring student went on her travels again and eventually went to live with her youngest brother.[63]

The twenty-three-year-old Constance Louisa Maynard, on a visit to an aunt in Scotland, also heard about Hitchin College and immediately longed to be a student there:

> It was a new world to me. I asked what 'Tripos' meant and how the students lived and a few other questions; and as we talked a quiet suggestion arose in my heart, as clear as a whisper from without, 'There, *that* is what you have been waiting for.' Aloud I said, 'How interesting! How I would like to go!' adding mentally in response to the voice 'Yes, yes, I won't disobey my parents in the last thing, but Oh! I'll move heaven and earth to get there'.[64]

It was only after she had been some time at home that she dared to introduce the subject, first of all to her father who frowned and smiled, asking 'But where's the *use*? What's it for?' He murmured about Constance staying at home and being like her sisters and even offered to buy a pony if the idea was abandoned. Eventually Mr Maynard gave in, suggesting that if Constance could obtain her mother's consent, the necessary bills for Hitchin would be paid. Mrs Maynard raised a number of objections but finally relented, asking her daughter not to take a degree after her year's study nor to take up teaching or get any ideas of leaving home. Constance promised anything and everything in order to win her mother's approval.[65]

In October 1873, Hitchin College was moved to a site much closer to Cambridge University, at Girton. Girton College was outside, rather than integrated into, the university structure and was founded on the principle of 'the same' education for women and men – which created many difficulties for the ill-prepared students such as Constance, who by this time had persuaded her parents to allow her to enter Girton and study for the Moral Sciences Tripos:

> Three years and one term was in those days the time allowed to men in which to take the Tripos, and Miss Emily Davies scorned all compromises and her students must conform to the same rule. She had an eye to the remote future when, she believed . . . Degrees (even retrospective ones) would be granted by the University of Cambridge to those who had fully complied with the conditions laid down for undergraduates.
>
> We trusted our leader, and that this would prove the right course in the end we never doubted, but that some individuals suffered

greatly by the working of these inexorable laws was equally clear. So of this first year's students, two fell off and three remained – three who, in spite of holes and gaps in their previous knowledge, in spite of the difficulty found in dealing with masses of new thought, which at times seemed to be overwhelming, struggled through to their goal; two to the Classical Tripos and one to the Mathematical Tripos.[66]

Some Girton students and tutors felt, however, that the social cost of Miss Davies' insistence on 'the same' higher education for women and men was high. Louisa Lumsden, a tutor at Girton for 'two lonely and difficult' years in the early 1870s believed that Miss Davies' views separated Louisa and even Miss Davies herself from social life in Cambridge and from another women's college that was founded in that city, Newnham College.[67]

Unlike Girton, Newnham was the outcome of principles based on the theme of 'separate and different' education for women. In the late 1860s the North of England Council, of which Anne Jemima Clough was secretary, were of the view that identical examinations for women and men were not desirable and thus a memorial was sent to Cambridge University asking for an examination for women over 18 years of age. The request was granted and in 1869, 36 candidates sat the examination.[68] In 1870, mainly through the efforts of Henry Sidgwick, a Cambridge don, special lectures for women were established in order to prepare them for the Women's Examinations. The students needed a place of residence and in 1871, Anne Clough was asked to take charge of a house at 74 Regent Street (Newnham Hall was not erected until 1876). From its very beginnings, therefore, Newnham was different in orientation to Girton. Whereas the latter wished to prove that women were capable of the 'same intellectual work as men', the former considered such a view 'undesirable' in the 'interest of the individual students' who were intellectually ill-prepared for such a hurdle.[69]

Such a compromising attitude towards women's education did not fully challenge the dominant ideal of middle-class femininity and therefore met with less fierce opposition than the Girton principles. Miss Clough encouraged the students to begin with 'familiar' subjects, such as arithmetic, history, English language and literature and to then take up whatever was of most interest.[70] Traditional middle-class ideas about femininity were evident also in the 'noble enthusiasm' for social service that flourished at Newnham where the students concerned themselves with the emancipation of their 'fellow underdogs, the working-classes, and had given lessons to groups of working men'.[71] Entry into the typically feminine occupation of schoolteaching was also encouraged. Indeed, oral tradition has it that Newnham was for governesses while Girton was for ladies and that generally, the former was further 'down-market' than the latter.[72] This was reflected in the differential fees and standards of accommodation in the two institutions. At Girton in 1875, where students had both bedrooms and sitting-rooms, the fees were £105 per annum while at Newnham, which only had single bed-sitting rooms, £60 a year was charged with an additional maximum of twelve guineas for tuition, such sums being reduced to £45 and six guineas, respectively, for those intending to become teachers.[73] Even the lower Newnham fees, however, would be beyond the means of most clever working-class women – who were also unlikely to be socialized into the mores considered suitable for college life. As Pedersen notes, only a few poor but able girls, some the daughters of tradesmen or artisan-tradesmen, managed to enter the universities and go on to teach. Indeed, Howarth and Curthoys point out that the total number of ex-elementary schoolgirls who went up to English and Welsh universities with scholarships in 1910 was 70; of these, 18 went to London, 3 to Cambridge and none to Oxford.[74]

Whatever their social background, the women students at Girton and Newnham were expected to be ladylike – since to behave otherwise was to risk the success of such pioneering ventures. In the early years of these colleges, the male university dons repeated to the women students the lectures delivered to their male undergraduates since it was considered 'improper' for lectures to be mixed (a practice that was later abolished). Yet even though the classes were single sex, chaperons were expected, sometimes with amusing results, as Mary Paley (later Marshall), an early Newnham student, recollected:

> Though the classes were not mixed, chaperons were necessary, and poor Miss Clough, having to do a good deal of this work, sometimes also went to sleep. At the end of a long economic argument she once woke up with 'Would you mind saying that over again Mr Marshall, it is so difficult', and he meekly obeyed.[75]

In addition, the least deviation, whether in manner or dress, from the ordinary rules of society was to be avoided. The main idea was to escape observation and to seem like a 'nice girl' who did not know too much.[76] In particular, Miss Clough was known for the various devices she used to delicately convey to the students her dislike of anything in their dress or appearance:

> If a girl wore shorter dresses than she liked, she would seize the opportunity of her wearing a slightly longer one to say how much she liked it, and why. If a girl wore her hair in a fringe (a fashion Miss Clough abhorred), she would put it aside with her hands and say, 'I like to see your forehead'.[77]

Smoking, of course, was prohibited since it was feared that parents would not send their daughters to Newnham if they thought such a 'masculine' habit would be acquired. Miss Clough, herself a smoker, was forced to retreat to a friend's smoking room whenever she wished to indulge the habit or else hire a hansom and drive out into the country.[78]

Although the early women students at Cambridge often resented such restrictions, they usually followed them, only too aware of their pioneering status as *new women* in higher education. Gradually, during the period up to 1914, many of the ladylike constraints were slowly eroded. But the struggle of women to win access to degree examinations, and to be awarded a degree, on equal terms with men, was a painstakingly slow process. In 1881, Cambridge University allowed women to sit the degree examinations but not to be awarded a degree. It is little wonder that even in the late 1890s, women students felt their presence to be 'more or less on sufferance'.[79] It was not until 1947 that the university finally capitulated and awarded women degrees on the same terms as men, 28 years after Oxford University had conceded on this issue.[80]

The struggle of women to be awarded degrees in other universities was won much earlier – at London University in 1878, the Victoria University in 1880, the Scottish universities in 1892 and the University of Durham in 1895.[81] This does not mean, of course, that women were fully accepted on equal terms with men nor fully integrated into the university structure. Edith Lang was one of the first four of Victoria's women graduates and studied for her degree at Owens College, Manchester. She and a female friend thought they were good at mathematics but although they pleaded hard to work for the B.Sc., they were told that 'a woman's brain was not equal to the higher mathematics'. So they 'meekly turned' to the study of classics, of which they knew nothing, and to history.[82] Furthermore, the women students at Owens were mainly contained within a separate Women's Department or Women's College in a 'grim old house' in Brunswick Street and could not go across to attend classes in Owens College itself until they had passed a preliminary exam. Entry into the Owens building was something of an ordeal:

> How awe-stricken my chum and I felt the first day we 'went across'! Not that we met with any worse treatment than being gazed at as if we were a new species; but, still, we were very glad when the first plunge was over . . . We had some curious unwritten etiquette. For instance, we never thought of entering Owens by the principal door, but always that to the right of the quad, and we were always ushered out of the History Theatre by the professor.[83]

Ladylike propriety demanded too that the women students could not enter the library and ask for a book. Instead, they had to fill in a voucher which was given to a maid-of-all-work, aged about 13, who went to the library with it. If the maid was unsure of the volume, she might have to make the library journey ten times.[84]

At London University also, women were expected to 'know' and 'keep' their place. When Marie Stopes (later famous as a birth control campaigner) attended University College in the early 1900s, she was amazed by the extent of prejudice against women. As president of the Women's Union Debating Society, she shocked the university authorities when she initiated joint debates with the men's union and chaired the first joint debate.[85] But the brilliant young student was undeterred by such reactions.

Marie soon discovered that, although an internal student, she could take an honours degree in one year instead of three if she sat as an external student – provided she gained honours in one subject and a first-class pass in the second. Taking the external route, she was the only candidate in November 1902 to gain a first class honours in botany and a third class in geology. The award of the university's Gilchrist Scholarship enabled her to undertake postgraduate study and in 1905 she became the youngest Doctor of Science in Britain.[86]

Marie Stopes and the other university women of her day were important role models for future generations of aspiring female scholars, especially those who still encountered parental and societal prejudice to their plans to enter higher education. Vera Brittain (later a feminist writer and pacifist) spent the time between

August 1913 and April 1914 preparing for the entrance examinations to Oxford University. The small provincial town of Buxton,
Derbyshire, was abuzz with her activity. 'Have you heard? Vera
Brittain's going to be a lecturer!'[87] Her mother was invariably
questioned by other middle-class mothers about her acquiescence
in abandoning all hope of finding her daughter a husband. ' "How
can you send your daughter to college, Mrs Brittain!" moaned
one lugubrious lady. "Don't you want her ever to get *married*?" [88]
The persistent belief that a woman's natural destiny was marriage
had to be fought against and the ideal established of the *new woman*
who could be a celibate careerist, professionally trained and
financially independent of a husband's economic support. However, since a number of the 'new' graduate women married this
helped to disprove, as Sara Delamont has aptly pointed out, the old
claim that no man wanted a graduate wife. In particular, from
the earliest days of college education the male lecturing staff had
'snatched the graduates away into marriage'. The educational
pioneers created therefore another new female role, continues
Delamont, the wife who was an intellectual partner to her husband,
an articulate companion 'who could swap Greek epigrams or
scientific formulae'.[89]

Despite the prejudices women students encountered in higher
education, many were jubilant about college life. Hertha Marks
(later the experimental physicist Hertha Ayrton), returning to
Girton in October 1877 after ill health had forced her to go down
for two terms, wrote enthusiastically to Barbara Bodichon who was
sponsoring her through college:

> Here I am in the dear old room again (the same that I had before),
> sitting at my study table and feeling as if I had never left it. It is very
> delightful to be back again, scrambling for breakfast, quizzing
> lecturers, and talking shop from morning till night![90]

Having a room of one's own, where studying could be continuous
rather than constantly interrupted by family duties when a daughter
at home, was especially welcomed. Winifred Peck, a student at
Lady Margaret Hall, Oxford, during the early twentieth century,
recalled:

> To know one was safe from the intrusions of friends, relatives and
> housemaids was freedom indeed. My sister and I had a sitting-
> room of our own at home, but we also shared a bedroom so that for
> the first time in my life I knew real privacy.[91]

Many students, such as Winifred Seebohm, hoping to learn self reliance, judgement and self-confidence were not disappointed.[92] Margaret Merrifield (later Verrall), a future classicist and psychical researcher, was a student at Newnham in the late 1870s. One day, in her Greek class, she was 'bold enough' to offer a new interpretation of a passage in the *Agamemnon*. Her tutor, Archer Hind, praised the suggestion and at first seemed keen to adopt it. Finally, however, he concluded that the ordinary interpretation was perhaps more in accordance with Aeschylean ideas, although one might bear Margaret's interpretation in mind. 'Wasn't that a triumph?' wrote home the buoyant student. 'After learning Greek about two months,' she continued, 'to strike out a new interpretation of the *Agamemnon* and be told that it was a good one! Shan't I get conceited?'[93]. As Williams notes, such small successes were important for the students, building up their confidence enormously.[94] Participation in college debates also taught students how to speak in public, sum up arguments, challenge an opposing view and present one's own case. In addition, as Vicinus has ably shown, college life with its corporate identity and sense of community could enable women students and staff to lead an independent intellectual life.[95]

The experience of higher education faciliated the entry of many women into certain forms of employment, and paid work became a legitimate area of activity for middle- and upper-class women, a goal to be aimed for, if desired. The entry of women into higher education had, therefore, profound implications for their subsequent social placement within the economic structure. By the beginning of the twentieth century, we find a new, educated, female elite who were concentrated in particular kinds of professional work. Among the students who took the Hygiene Course at Bedford College, for example, was Maud Hartland, who became in 1913 one of the first woman Inspectors under the National Insurance Act; Kerstin Hesselgren, the first woman Factory Inspector in Sweden, first woman member of the Senate of the Riksdag and a member of the Swedish Delegation to the Thirteenth Assembly of the League of Nations; Hilda Martindale, who became Deputy Chief Inspector of Factories in 1921 and then Director of Women's Establishments, HM Treasury (1933–7); Sumi Miyakawa, who became Head of the School of Domestic Economy, Tokyo; Irene Whitworth, who in 1916 was appointed Assistant Director, Welfare and Health Department, Ministry of Munitions.[96]

However, this new female elite was especially concentrated in teaching posts in the expanding fee-paying schools for middle-class girls established by the Girls' Public Day School Trust. Thus ex-Newnham students such as Edith Creak and Frances Gray became headmistresses – the former at a GPDST school in Brighton and the latter at St Paul's Girls' School.[97] The presence of such well-educated teachers within the GPDST schools helped to increase the pool of recruits for the women's colleges and thus a cyclical relationship was established between the two kinds of educational institution.[98] Generally, college educated women avoided teaching in the state-financed, elementary sector that catered almost exclusively for working-class children; there was indeed much debate about whether it was 'genteel' for middle-class women to enter elementary schoolteaching.[99] Some of the women students in higher education eventually became college or university lecturers themselves. Miss Welsh, a Girton student, became a mistress at that college from 1885–1904 while Margaret Murray, a student in the 1890s of Egyptology at University College, London, became a member of the academic staff there.[100] The number of college educated women entering occupations in industry and business was very small.[101]

Overall, as Pedersen comments, the reforms in women's secondary and higher education in nineteenth-century England gave liberally educated women an edge in competing with other women for plum positions in occupations long open to women, especially schoolteaching, rather than encouraging large numbers of women to compete with men for less conventional employments.[102] The entry of middle-class women into higher education then served to polarize the differences between this educated female elite and other women, especially working-class women.

References

 1 Kelly (1962), p. 113.
 2 Quoted in Burstyn (1980), p. 126.
 3 Ibid., p. 126.
 4 Porter (1922), pp. 14–16.
 5 Ibid., pp. 20–23, p. 28, p. 31, p. 41.
 6 Ibid., p. 67, p. 71.
 7 Stephen (1927), p. 261.

8 National Association for the Promotion of Social Science, *Transactions* (1879), list of contents.

9 *Census of Great Britain, Education (England and Wales) 1851*, pp. 215–21.

10 Manchester Mechanics' Institution, *Annual Report* (1846), p. ix.

11 Quoted in Purvis (1989), p. 135.

12 Ibid., pp. 137–8.

13 Ibid., p. 134.

14 Manchester Mechanics' Institution (1863) *Thirty-Ninth Annual Report*, p. 13. By 1868, the curriculum in these classes included the 3Rs, advanced arithmetic, English Grammar, composition, geography, algebra, geometry, bookkeeping and English history – although the main demand was for the 'simpler studies, viz. Reading, Writing and Arithmetic'. Manchester Mechanics' Institution (1868) *Forty-Fourth Annual Report*, p. 12.

15 Quoted in Purvis (1989), p. 151.

16 Ibid., p. 182.

17 Steer (1962), p. 7.

18 B. and P. Russell (1937), p. 330.

19 Quoted in Purvis (1989), p. 155.

20 Quoted in ibid., p. 156.

21 Shepherd (ed.) 1870, pp. 86–7.

22 Purvis (1989), p. 178.

23 Quoted in ibid., p. 180.

24 Supplement to *The Working Men's College Magazine* 1 April 1859, p. 80; 'Afternoon classes for women' 1859, p. 125.

25 *The Working Men's College Magazine* 1 March 1860, p. 37.

26 *The Working Men's College Magazine* 1 October 1860, p. 164; Bibby (1955–6), p. 214.

27 Supplement to *The Working Men's College Magazine* 1 April 1859, p. 7.

28 Quoted in Purvis (1989), p. 211.

29 Raikes (1908), pp. 297–8.

30 Quoted in Purvis (1989), pp. 212–13.

31 Jenkins (1953), p. 38.

32 Ibid., p. 119.

33 Stott (1978), p. 10.

34 Quoted in ibid., p. 24.

35 Ibid., p. 24.

36 Martindale (1944), p. 31.

37 Anderson (1987), p. 26, p. 42.

38 Kelly (1962), p. 228.

39 Muir (1950), p. 147–8.

40 Percival (1939), p. 124.

41 Ibid., p. 14.
42 Tuke (1939), p. 24, p. 34.
43 Ibid., pp. 29–35.
44 Raikes (1908), p. 25.
45 Quoted in Grylls (1948), p. 35.
46 Stuart (1911), pp. 157–8.
47 Ibid., p. 162.
48 Ibid., p. 162.
49 Quoted in Jepson (1973), p. 104.
50 Roberts (1891), p. 13.
51 Carpenter (1916), p. 80.
52 Roberts (1891), p. 14.
53 Rowbotham (1981), p. 71, suggests that the small number of working-class women who did become students in university extension classes were mainly pupil-teachers in elementary schools.
54 Foley (1973), p. 46.
55 Fletcher (1989), p. 64, notes that, despite the fact that the university extension movement had developed out of the movement for women's education, that many of its most influential figures were sympathetic to the women's cause, and that at least two thirds of its students were women, 'there had always been strong resistance to appointing women as lecturers'. Maude Royden (1876–1956), the subject of Fletcher's biography, was the first woman to be invited (in 1903)) by the Oxford University Extension Delegacy to be one of their lecturers.
56 Quoted in Kelly (1962), p. 227.
57 Carpenter (1916), p. 84.
58 Quoted in Jepson (1973), p. 105; Whibley (1894), p. 599.
59 Stephen (1927), p. 189. For Emily Davies' objections to 'separate schemes for women' see the same source, p. 195.
60 Extract from Sewell's *Women and the Times We Live In* (1868), reprinted in Murray (1984), p. 213.
61 Davies (1866), p. 510.
62 'The profession of an English matron' (1871), p. 627.
63 Lloyd (1928), pp. 50–51.
64 Firth (1949), p. 93.
65 Ibid., pp. 102–3.
66 Maynard (1910), pp. 180–1.
67 Lumsden (1933), p. 58.
68 Clough (1897), pp. 129–30.
69 Ibid., p. 175.
70 Ibid., p. 169.
71 Glendinning (1969), p. 52.
72 Sutherland (1987), p. 100.
73 Ibid., p. 102.

74 Pedersen (1987), p. 224; Howarth and Curthoys (1987), p. 12 footnote 5.
75 Marshall (1947), p. 15.
76 Maynard (1910) p. 190.
77 Clough (1897), p. 240.
78 Phillips (ed.) 1979, p. 45.
79 Ibid., p. 38.
80 For accounts of the history of the women's colleges at Oxford University see especially Rogers (1938) and Brittain (1960).
81 Sidgwick (1901), p. 203.
82 Lang (1901), p. 56.
83 Ibid., p. 56.
84 Ibid., pp. 56–8.
85 Hall (1977), p. 36.
86 Ibid., pp. 32–4.
87 Brittain (1933), p. 72.
88 Ibid., p. 73.
89 Delamont (1978b), p. 182, p. 184.
90 Sharp (1926), pp. 63–4.
91 Peck (1952), p. 156.
92 Glendinning (1969), p. 87.
93 Phillips (ed) 1979, p. 8.
94 Williams (1987), p. 178.
95 Vicinus (1985), Chapter 4.
96 Tuke (1939), pp. 159–60.
97 Hamilton (1936), p. 114.
98 Purvis (1981c), p. 370.
99 Widdowson (1980), Purvis (1981c).
100 Stephen (1927), p. 314; Murray (1963), pp. 93–6.
101 Sanderson (1972), pp. 328–9.
102 Pederson (1987), p. 378.

CHAPTER 6

Echoes into the Late Twentieth Century

As we have seen throughout this book, social class and gender differentiation helped to shape the forms and content of female education in England from 1800 to 1914. Although such divisions are not so striking today, they are still evident and echo into the late twentieth century. Rather than offer a brief chronological account of female education from 1914 to the present, I shall focus upon a few key themes that illustrate the importance of history for the understanding of contemporary events.

A centralized curriculum revisited? A historical perspective on the National Curriculum for state-educated girls

Many commentators to-day see similarities between past government attempts to impose a centralized curriculum on state maintained schools and the changes introduced by a Tory government in the 1980s.[1] As we saw in Chapter 2, in 1862 Robert Lowe, a member of a government keen to reduce expenditure on elementary schooling for the working classes, introduced the Revised Code whereby all future grants, apart from building, were to be based on a payment of 12s. per pupil per annum and were subject to certain conditions; in particular, part of the grant was dependent upon the pupil reaching a satisfactory standard in a limited range of subjects – reading, writing and arithmetic – with plain needlework for girls only. Although 'payment by results' (as the system was called) was officially abolished in 1900, the idea of a centrally directed curriculum was extended to state secondary schools (established by the 1902 Act) through the 1904 Board of Education

Regulations which prescribed the syllabus for pupils up to the ages of sixteen or seventeen. Gradually, however, the government relaxed its tight control and direction of school curricula – by the late 1920s for state elementary schools and by 1944 for state secondary schools. Such a development was strengthened by the 1944 Education Act which established a 'partnership' between central government, teachers and local education authorities, even though the balance of power and responsibilities was never evenly distributed.[2]

A return to a strong regulatory centralized framework for state education is to be found, once again, in the late twentieth century.[3] In particular, the 1988 Education Reform Act requires that a National Curriculum be implemented in all state maintained schools. This will involve core subjects of English, maths and science, and foundation subjects of technology and design, history, geography, music, art, physical education, a modern foreign language (for secondary schools only) plus compulsory religious education. Attainment targets will be set for each subject and pupils will be assessed regularly at 7, 11, 14 and 16 years. As will be obvious from earlier statements in this chapter, such a centralized curriculum, with built-in test procedures for all state educated children, is not 'new'. As Horn reminds us, a 'national' or 'core' curriculum was first implemented in England and Wales over a century ago.[4]

The term *National* Curriculum in the 1990s, however, is a misnomer, just as it is when applied to the 1860s. In the 1860s, middle-class girls educated outside the state sector were untouched by the system of payment by results. In the 1990s, fee-paying independent schools, where girls make up only 6% of the total of all children of school age,[5] are excluded from the legislative imposition of the National Curriculum. As in the past, fee-paying independent schools enjoy more prestige than free state schools, partly because the level of fees ensures that the clientele are drawn mainly from the middle and wealthier classes of society. In particular, girls' independent boarding schools to-day with annual fees from £3,300 to £6,300, usually attract a wealthy international clientele while the girls' private day schools, with annual charges from £1,500 to £4,050, often draw on a local middle-class population.[6] Not unexpectedly, the most prestigious private girls' schools are the expensive boarding schools with strong roots in the nineteenth century, such as Roedean and Cheltenham Ladies'

College, drawing almost exclusively from the ranks of the upper middle class.

It is, perhaps, in the continued existence of both private and state maintained schools, which form two very different and unequal sectors of education, that we can clearly see how social class still exerts a powerful influence on girls' schooling to-day. Since the 1980s legislation does not apply to independent schools, it implies, at the very least, that our society is divided into 'two nations' rather than one.[7] Tory education policy in the 1980s has thus served further to revisit and reinforce that differentiation between privately and state educated schoolgirls so common in the nineteenth century, namely a broad *education* for an elite as opposed to the much narrower *schooling* for the majority.

The changes introduced in the 1980s pose, however, not only new challenges for those concerned with class inequalities in education but also in regard to gender differentiation and the increasingly important area of race. Theoretically, since state educated boys *and* girls now have access to a common rather than gender-specific curriculum, this should help to eliminate sex inequality in schools; in particular, the disappearance of that traditional 'feminine' subject, home economics, could bring many advantages to girls.[8] However, not everyone is convinced that the National Curriculum should be welcomed as a means of promoting equal opportunities for schoolgirls.

Arnot believes that despite the 'golden opportunities' found in the possibility of all girls studying those subjects commonly associated with boys, such as science and technology, the prevailing message of the National Curriculum could be just the reverse of encouraging social equality. It could confirm girls' sense of themselves as 'second class' in a world where female subjects such as domestic science and child care are not compulsory and hence low status, and where the spheres in which boys excel and the teachers are predominantly male have high status. Similarly, Miles and Middleton fear that equal access to a common curriculum is insufficient for guaranteeing equal treatment in the classroom and in the wider society outside.[9] Other commentators warn that the co-educational nature of state maintained schools disadvantages girls since mixed schools are really boys' schools with girls fitted into a male paradigm.[10]

Social status and cultural capital retained? A historical perspective on girls' private schools

As we saw in Chapter 4, the education of upper- and middle-class girls from 1800–1914 was sharply differentiated from that of the majority of girls attending state schools. This was especially so after the 1870s when academic fee-paying girls' schools were established, offering a curriculum of high status academic knowledge, ladylike accomplishments and games. A brief examination of girls' private schooling today reveals many telling parallels with the past.

Girls' independent schools today have retained the function of imparting to their pupils the cultural capital of the middle and upper classes. Although the academic standards within such schools are variable, it is in such institutions, outside the constraints of the National Curriculum, that girls have access to such high status subjects as the classics, to typically middle-class pursuits such as lacrosse, ballet, fencing and riding, and to various 'ladylike' accomplishments such as flower arranging and playing the piano, violin or guitar.[11] Indeed, the emphasis upon becoming a *ladylike home-maker*, a dominant ideal for middle-class girls in the past, has not been entirely abandoned.

Blandford suggested in the 1970s that, with a few exceptions, the majority of girls' boarding schools are primarily concerned with teaching those social and educational skills that will make their pupils into 'ladies' who will value success through marriage rather than through academic achievement.[12] Although evaluation of such statements is difficult since the topic has not been adequately researched, there is limited evidence to support such assertions.

Caroline St John-Brooks, a pupil at a girls' boarding school at Bath in the 1950s, found that the aim seemed to be to produce 'nice wives for army officers' with 'prowess on the lacrosse field' mattering more than exam passes.[13] Okely reiterates that scholarly achievements and higher education in her boarding school were reserved only for a few girls, possibly marked as vocational spinsters. Despite her academic credentials of 13 'O' levels and while studying for four 'A' levels, she received little encouragement to progress further. Indeed, the senior mistress told her that she would be 'selfish' to go to university, thereby depriving someone worthier of a place. Instead, she was advised to make use of her 'A' levels in French and Art by training as a designer of corsets and lingerie for a famous company in Switzerland![14] Okely believes that while *some* middle-class girls attend private schools which encourage independent careers there are other middle- or upper-class girls who are denied this, *precisely because of their class*. The development for them of a distinct class consciousness is seen as more important than scholarship and achievement.[15] Such views are supported by Delamont who asserts that 'many' girls' private schools to-day have betrayed the 'campaigning zeal' of the nineteenth-century women pioneers; the trap of double conformity to both male academic standards and ladylike behaviour has now become an end in itself rather than a means to an end.[16]

Nevertheless, those girls' schools to-day that do encourage scholastic achievement continue that tradition of academic excellence carefully nurtured by the nineteenth-century reforming headmistresses, such as Miss Buss and Miss Beale. Thus Delamont found amongst the 14- and 15-year olds in an expensive girls' boarding school in East Scotland, a group of eleven girls who called themselves 'the academic set – the intellectuals'; they were studious, had intellectual hobbies, hated team games and were more likely than the other pupils to belong to the Girl Guides, to choirs and orchestras outside the school, and to play musical instruments. Even the group of twelve girls heavily involved in adolescent culture and called 'the debs and dollies' by the academic set, were not failing academically. Whereas many of the academic set wished to attend Oxford or Cambridge rather than a local university, and follow a career which stretched beyond a first degree into research, many of the debs and dollies hoped to enter more typically female professions such as social work and teaching small children.[17] Wober in a survey of 23 girls' boarding schools in England also found that being 'good at work, an outstanding scholar' was rated as the most important aspiration amongst the pupils.[18]

Women in adult and higher education today – still separate and unequal?

A brief examination of the nature of women's education today also reveals some interesting comparisons with the past. As we saw in Chapter 3, adult education in the nineteenth century was often organized by the middle classes for those in the 'lower' orders of society, and especially for working-class men. Those working-class women who successfully struggled to enter male oriented educational movements were usually carefully segregated into single sex classes and offered a basic curriculum of the 3Rs and certain domestic skills, such as plain sewing. Such a class and gender specific curriculum was shaped by middle-class ideas about the appropriate role in society for working-class women, namely that they should be educated to become good wives and mothers.

Today, however, in contrast to the past, the majority of students in adult education are women; furthermore, the social class background of these women is now predominately middle rather than working class.[19] For example, women students today in the wide range of recreative adult education classes provided by the local education authorities (LEAs) are mainly drawn from the lower ranks of the middle class while that smaller number found in the more academic courses run by university extension centres (usually called extra mural departments) and the Workers' Educational Association tend to come from more solidly middle-class backgrounds.[20] Yet, despite these contrasts with the past, the most popular of the range of courses for women students in adult education today include those subjects so familiar to historians of women's history, namely various 'homecrafts' such as dressmaking, cookery and cake icing.[21] It would appear that women's choices in adult education are still constrained by ideas about their femininity.

Higher education in the nineteenth century, as we saw in Chapter 5, was associated with the middle classes, and especially middle-class men. Yet a minority of middle-class women fought successfully to enter the universities and to be awarded degrees on the same terms as men. The number of full time women students in higher education has steadily grown in the twentieth century so that in the United Kingdom in 1987/8 they numbered nearly 281,000 compared with 346,000 full time men.[22] But such expansion has consolidated rather than substantially diminished the traditional social class composition of the student body. In particular, working-class women still do not enter higher education in large numbers, especially the more 'elite' institutions, the universities. 80% of all students accepted for university places in 1988 were from professional and skilled white collar backgrounds with only 12.5% from skilled manual, 6.3% from partly skilled and 1.1% from unskilled homes.[23]

Some higher educational institutions today, especially the polytechnics, are now trying to widen the social band from which their students are drawn by offering places to mature entrants who, instead of possessing the traditional entry requirements of Advanced Level Examinations, have passes in 'second chance' or 'access' courses. However, not all women 'non-standard' entrants, especially those with responsibilities for young children, welcome the male, white, middle-class ethos of higher education.[24] Since key posts in higher educational institutions are largely held by men,[25] policy decisions are made in men's interests. Thus adequate and secure funding is given for some facilities, such as sports and upkeep of gardens, and not for others, such as nurseries. As Lees and Scott point out, in many institutions of higher education, no budget is allocated to the nursery and any shortfall from fees is expected to be made good through fund raising events such as jumble sales.[26]

Once in higher education, female and male students tend to follow different educational routes: the women are mainly concentrated in the typically 'feminine' subjects, such as the arts and languages, the men in the biological and physical sciences, business and social studies, engineering and technology. In these tendencies, as in much else, we can see reflections from the past. Indeed, overall it would be fair to say that the patterns of social class and gender differentiation established in girls' and women's education in the Victorian and Edwardian eras are still echoing in England today.

References

1 See, for example, Horn (1987), Aldrich (1988) and Brehony (1990).
2 Bogdanor (1979).
3 For discussion of this point see, for example, the various chapters in Flude and Hammer (eds) 1990.
4 Horn (1987), p. 29. Aldrich (1988), p. 22, dates the first attempt to impose a 'national' curriculum back to 1904 rather than the 1860s.
5 Griffin (ed.) 1990, p. 54.
6 Ayer (1989), p. 31.
7 Aldrich (1988), p. 29, raises the issue of what concept of a nation underlies the National Curriculum and asks a number of questions, such as the following. Is it that teachers in independent schools can be trusted to provide 'a balanced curriculum and appropriate standards of education' whilst teachers in state schools cannot? It is that pupils in independent schools can be trusted 'to make the right choice of

subjects and to work hard' whilst those in state schools cannot? Are independent schools 'to be above the law'?

8 Some of the components of home economics will be absorbed into some subjects within the National Curriculum, namely design and technology, and personal, social and health education. Attar (1990) p. 148 argues that home economics should be taken apart 'for good', and seen as a piece of history which should no longer be allowed 'to shackle' girls' and boys' education.

9 Arnot (1989), p. 8; Miles and Middleton (1990). Weiner (1989), p. 121, however, points out that the concern with equal opportunities in new governmental vocational initiatives in schools may allow a stronger institutional base than ever before for equal opportunities work.

10 For general discussions about the disadvantages and advantages of co-education for girls see, for example, Arnot (1983), the various contributions to Deem (ed.) 1983 and Burgess (1990).

11 See, for example, the 1990 prospectus for Lavant House, Chichester, West Sussex; Portsmouth High School for Girls; Roedean and Cheltenham Ladies' College.

12 Blandford (1977).

13 St John-Brooks (1988), p. 12.

14 Okely (1983), p. 213 (first pub. 1979).

15 Ibid., p. 209.

16 Delamont (1989), pp. 176-7.

17 Delamont (1967), pp. 38-9.

18 Wober (1971), p. 79.

19 Thompson (1983), p. 61; Bird (1991). As noted in the Introduction to this book, discussing the social class position of women is highly problematic since present day as well as nineteenth-century classifications of social class are mainly based upon the occupations of men.

20 Thompson (1983), p. 64. Adult education covers a much wider range of provision than just these forms mentioned, e.g. trade union provision, classes run by the Townswomen's Guild and the National Federation of Women's Institutes. See, for example, the interesting discussion offered by Deem (1983) in her study of four women's organizations and clubs – a flower arranging club, a branch of the Women's Institute, a women's club and a group forming part of the Women's Section of the Labour party.

21 Bird (1991). Bird points out that whereas the function of the domestic curriculum for working-class women in the nineteenth century was seen as remedial, the homecrafts emphasis for middle-class women in adult education today is seen as adding to the quality of leisure. The other most popular group of subjects for women in adult education covers a range of physical education activities, such as keep fit, dancing and various sports.

22 Griffin (ed.) 1990, p. 59.

23 UCCA (1989), p. 4.

24 See, for example, the critique offered by the Taking Liberties Collective (1989). The fifty-seven women forming the collective, all but one or two from the working class and living on low wages or state support, experienced many difficulties. The following comment (p. 32) from one such 'non-standard' entrant, attempting to balance the double shift of home responsibilities and student's life is not atypical – 'All of us went through a cracking up period. One after another we went down with crying fits, mostly due to exhaustion, feelings of not belonging, not knowing what was expected, trying to read too many unreadable books in a week and listening to incomprehensible, obscure or plain old boring lectures hour after hour, that had no relevance to our lives and simply made us feel put down or knackered from having to rush home at 3.00 to sort out children, cook dinners, clean houses and trying to write essays at midnight, mostly wondering why the hell we ever wanted to be there in the first place.'

25 Hansard Commission Society Report (1990), p. 65, notes that amongst full-time non-clinical university staff women from only 3% of professors, 6% of senior lecturers, 14% of lecturers.

26 Lees and Scott (1990).

Bibliography

'Afternoon classes for women' (1859). *The Working Men's College Magazine*, 1 August.

Aldrich, R. (1988). 'The National Curriculum: an historical perspective' in D. Lawson and C. Chitty (eds) *The National Curriculum*. London, Bedford Way Paper 33, Institute of Education, University of London.

Allsop, G. (1987). *Reminiscences of a Manchester Woman*. Stockton on Tees, Janice Owen.

Anderson, K. (1950). 'Frances Mary Buss, the founder as headmistress' in M. Scrimgeour (ed.) *The North London Collegiate School 1850–1950, A Hundred Years of Girls' Education*. London, Oxford University Press.

Anderson, N.F. (1987). *Woman Against Women in Victorian England, A Life of Eliza Lynn Linton*. Bloomington and Indianapolis, Indiana University Press.

Arnot, M. (1983). 'A cloud over co-education: an analysis of the forms of transmission of class and gender relations' in S. Walker and L. Barton (eds) *Gender, Class and Education*. Lewes, Falmer Press.

Arnot, M. (1989). 'Crisis or challenge: equal opportunities and the National Curriculum' *NUT Education Review, Equal Opportunities in the New ERA*, Vol. 3, No. 2, Autumn.

Athill, D. (1965) (first pub. 1963). *Instead of a Letter*. London, The Reprint Society.

Attar, D. (1990). *Wasting Girls' Time, The History and Politics of Home Economics*. London, Virago Press.

Ayer, J. (1989). 'Bed, board – and an education to boot' *The Observer*, Sunday 12 March.

Bamford, T.W. (1975). 'Thomas Arnold and the Victorian idea of a public school' in B. Simon and I. Bradley (eds) *The Victorian Public School*. Dublin, Gill and Macmillan.

Banks, O. (1981). *Faces of Feminism*. Oxford, Martin Robertson.

Barlee, E. (1863). *A Visit to Lancashire in December, 1863*. London, Seeley, Jackson & Halliday.

Bates, H. and Wells, A.A.M. (1962). *A History of Shrewsbury High School 1885–1960*. Shrewsbury, Wilding and Sons.

Beddoe, D. (1983). *Discovering Women's History*. London, Pandora Press.

Bell, E. Moberley. (1942). *Octavia Hill*. London, Constable and Co.

Bennett, D. (1990). *Emily Davies and the Liberation of Women*. London, Andre Deutsch.

Bibby, C. (1955–6). 'The South London Working Men's College, a forgotten venture' *Adult Education*, 28.

Birchenough, C (1914). *History of Elementary Education in England and Wales from 1800 to the Present Day*. London, University Tutorial Press.

Bird, L. (1991). 'To cook or to conjugate: gender and class in the adult curriculum 1865–1900' *Gender and Education*, Vol. 3, No. 2.

Black, N. (1989). *Social Feminism*. Ithaca and London, Cornell University Press.

Blandford, L. (1977). 'The making of a lady' in G. Fraser MacDonald (ed.) *The World of the Public School*. London, Weidenfeld and Nicholson.

Blaszak, B.J. (1986). 'The Women's Cooperative Guild, 1883–1921' *International Social Science Review*, Vol. 61, No. 2.

Blunden, G. (1984). 'Vocational education for women's work in England and Wales' in S. Acker, J. Megarry, S. Nisbet and E. Hoyle (eds) *World Yearbook of Education 1984: Women and Education*, London, Kogan Page.

Board of Education (1926). *Report of the Consultative Committee on The Education of the Adolescent*. London, HMSO.

Bogdanor, V. (1979). 'Power and participation' *Oxford Review of Education*, Vol. 5, No. 2.

Booth, Rev. Dr J. (1855). *On the Female Education of the Industrial Classes; being the substance of a lecture delivered on the 20th November 1855, at the Mechanics' Institution, Wandsworth*. London, Bell and Daldy.

Bowerman, E. (1966). *Stands There a School*. Brighton, privately printed.

Brehony, K.J. (1990). 'Neither rhyme nor reason: primary schooling and the National Curriculum' in M. Flude and M. Hammer (eds) *The Education Reform Act 1988, Its Origins and Implications*. Lewes, Falmer Press.

Bremner, C.S. (1897). *Education of Girls and Women in Great Britain*. London, Swan Sonnenschein and Co.

British and Foreign School Society (1822). *Seventeenth Report of the British and Foreign School Society*. London, R. and A. Taylor.

British and Foreign School Society (1833). *Twenty-eighth Report of the British and Foreign School Society*. London, S. Bagster Jun.

Brittain, V. (1933). *Testament of Youth, An Autobiographical Study of the Years 1900–1925*. London, Victor Gollancz.

Brittain, V. (1960). *The Women at Oxford, A Fragment of History*. London, George Harrap.

Bryant, M. (1979). *The Unexpected Revolution: A Study in the Education of Women and Girls in the Nineteenth Century*. London, University of London Institute of Education.

Bryant, S. (1900). 'Retrospect: The North Collegiate School for Girls' In E.M. Hill (ed.) with the co-operation of S. Bryant *Frances Mary Buss Schools' Jubilee Record*. London, Swan Sonnenschein.

Bunting, E.M., Bunting, D.E.L., Barnes, A.E. and Gardiner, B. (1907). *A School for Mothers*. London, Horace Marshall & Son.

Burgess, A. (1990). 'Co-education – the disadvantages for schoolgirls' *Gender and Education*, Vol. 2, No. 1.

Burnett, J. (ed.) (1982). *Destiny Obscure, Autobiographies of Childhood, Education and Family from the 1820s to the 1920s*. London, Allen Lane.

Burstall, S. (1933). *Retrospect & Prospect: Sixty Years of Women's Education*. London, Longmans, Green and Co.

Burstall, S. (1938). *Frances Mary Buss, An Educational Pioneer*. London, Society for Promoting Christian Knowledge.

Burstyn, J. (1980). *Victorian Education and the Ideal of Womanhood*. London, Croom Helm.

Butts, M. (1988). *The Crystal Cabinet, My Childhood at Salterns*. Manchester, Carcanet Press.

Caine, B. (1986). *Destined to be Wives, The Sisters of Beatrice Webb*. Oxford, Clarendon Press.

Carpenter, E. (1916). *My Days and Dreams*. London, Allen and Unwin.

Census of Great Britain, 1851.

Central Society of Education (1837). *Schools for the Industrious Classes*. London, Taylor and Walton.

Chew, D. Nield (1982). *Ada Nield Chew, The Life and Writings of a Working Woman*. London, Virago.

Chorley, K. (1950). *Manchester Made Them*. London, Faber and Faber.

Clarke, A.K. (1953). *A History of the Cheltenham Ladies' College 1853–1953*. London, Faber and Faber.

Clough, B.A. (1897). *A Memoir of Anne Jemima Clough*. London, Edward Arnold.

Cobbe, F.P. (1894) (3rd edn.). *Life of Frances Power Cobbe*. 2 volumes. London, Richard Bentley & Son.

Cole, M. (1949). *Growing Up Into Revolution*. London, Longmans, Green and Co.

Collet, C. (1892). 'Secondary education in London (girls)' in A.H.D. Acland and H. Llewellyn Smith (eds) *Studies in Secondary Education*. London, Percival and Co.

Committee of Council on Education, *Minutes 1840–41*, *Minutes 1841–2*.

[Communicated by the Senior Tutor] (1859). 'History of the Halifax Working Men's College', *The Working Men's College Magazine*, 1 October.

Countess of Warwick (ed.) (1898). *Joseph Arch, The Story of his Life Told by Himself*. London, Hutchinson and Co.

Cowan, I.R. (1968). ' "Mechanics" institutes and science and art classes in Salford in the nineteenth century' *The Vocational Aspect of Education*, 20.

Cross, E. (1950). 'Reminiscences of the school in its early years' in R.M. Scrimgeour (ed.) *The North London Collegiate School 1850–1950*. London, Oxford University Press.

Crow, D. (1977). *The Edwardian Woman*. London, Allen and Unwin.

Cuthbert, E.M. (1953). *Laurel Bank School 1903–1953*. Glasgow, John Smith and Son.

Dallas, G. (1978). 'Introduction' to 1978 edition (first pub. 1915) of Davies, M. Llewelyn (ed.). *Maternity, Letters from Working Women*. London, Virago.

David, M.E. (1980). *The State, The Family and Education*. London, Routledge & Kegan Paul.

Davidoff, L. (1973). *The Best Circles, Society Etiquette and the Season*. London, Croom Helm.

Davidoff, L., L'Esperance, J. and Newby, H. (1976). 'Landscape with figures: home and community in English society', in J. Mitchell and A. Oakley (eds) *The Rights and Wrongs of Women*. Harmondsworth, Penguin Books.

Davidoff, L. and Hall, C. (1987). *Family Fortunes, Men and Women of the English Middle Class 1780–1850*. London, Hutchinson.

Davies, E. (1864). 'On secondary instruction as relating to girls' (read at the Annual Meeting of the National Association for the Promotion of Social Science), reprinted in E. Davies (1910). *Thoughts on Some Questions Relating to Women, 1860–1908*. Cambridge, Bowes and Bowes.

(Davies, J.) (1866). 'Female education' *Quarterly Review*, no. 119.

(Davies, J.) (1869). 'Female education' *Quarterly Review*, April.

Davies, M. Llewelyn (1904). *The Women's Co-operative Guild, 1883–1904*. Kirby, Lonsdale.

Davies, M. Llewelyn (ed.). (1931). *Life As We Have Known It by Co-operative Working Women*. London, Hogarth Press.

Davin, A. (1978). 'Imperialism and motherhood'. *History Workshop*, 5, Spring.

Davin, A. (1979). ' "Mind that you do as you are told": reading books for Board School girls' *Feminist Review*, 3.

Deem, R. (1983). 'Gender, patriarchy and class in the popular education of women' in S. Walker and L. Barton (eds) *Gender, Class and Education*. Lewes, Falmer Press.

Deem, R. (ed.) (1983). *Co-education Reconsidered*. Milton Keynes, Open University Press.

Delamont, S. (1967). 'The girls most likely to: cultural reproduction and Scottish elites' *Scottish Journal of Sociology*, 1.

Delamont, S. (1978a). 'The contradictions in ladies' education', in

S. Delamont and L. Duffin (eds) (1975). *The Nineteenth-Century Woman, her Cultural and Physical World*. London, Croom Helm.

Delamont, S. (1978b). 'The domestic ideology and women's education', in S. Delamont and L. Duffin (eds) (1978). *The Nineteenth-Century Woman, Her Cultural and Physical World*. London, Croom Helm.

Delamont, S. (1989). *Knowledgeable Women, Structuralism and the Reproduction of Elites*. London, Routledge.

Detrosier, R. (1829). *An Address Delivered at the New Mechanics' Institution*. Manchester, T. Forrest.

Dick, M. (1980). 'The myth of the working-class Sunday school' *History of Education*, Vol. 9, No. 1.

Digby, A. (1982). 'New schools for the middle class girl' in P. Searby (ed.) *Educating the Victorian Middle Class*. Leicester, History of Education Society, Proceedings of the 1981 Annual Conference of the History of Education Society of Great Britain.

Dobbs, A.E. (1919). *Education and Social Movements 1700–1850*. London, Longmans, Green and Co.

Dove, I. (1988). *Yours in the Cause, A Brief Account of Suffragettes in Lewisham, Greenwich and Woolwich*. London, Lewisham Library Services and Greenwich Libraries.

Dunckley, H. (ed.) (1893). *Bamford's Passages in the Life of a Radical and Early Days*. 2 volumes. London, Fisher Unwin.

Duppa, B.F. (1839). *A Manual for Mechanics' Institutions*. London, Longman, Orme, Brown, Green and Longmans.

Dyhouse, C. (1981). *Girls Growing Up in Late Victorian and Edwardian England*. London, Routledge and Kegan Paul.

Dyhouse, C. (1987). 'Miss Buss and Miss Beale: gender and authority in the history of education' in F. Hunt (ed.) *Lessons for Life, The Schooling of Girls and Women 1850–1950*. Oxford, Basil Blackwell.

Ellis, Mrs S. (1839). *The Women of England: their relative duties, domestic influence, and social obligations*. London, Fisher, Son and Co.

Ellis, Mrs S. (1842). *The Daughters of England: their position in society, character and responsibilities*. London, Fisher, Son and Co.

Ellis, Mrs S. (1843). *The Wives of England, Their Relative Duties, Domestic Influence, & Social Obligations*. London, Fisher, Son and Co.

Englishwoman's Review, 15 October 1877.

Englishwoman's Review, 15 November 1880.

Englishwoman's Review, 15 January 1884.

Enquire Within Upon Everything (94th edn., revised) (1898). London, Houlston and Sons.

Farningham, M. (1907). *A Working Woman's Life*. London, James Clarke and Co.

Fletcher, S. (1980). *Feminists and Bureaucrats, a Study in the Development of Girls' Education in the Nineteenth Century*. Cambridge, Cambridge University Press.

Fletcher, S. (1989). *Maude Royden, A Life*. Oxford, Basil Blackwell.

Firth, C.B. (1949). *Constance Louisa Maynard, Mistress of Westfield College*. London, George Allen and Unwin.

Flude, M. and Hammer, M. (eds) (1990). *The Education Reform Act 1988, Its Origins and Implications*. Lewes, Falmer Press.

Foakes, G. (1976). *My Part of the River*. London, Futura.

Foley, A. (1973). *A Bolton Childhood*. Manchester, Manchester University Extra-Mural Department and the North Western District of the Workers' Educational Association.

Fraser, Mrs H. (1911). *A Diplomatist's Wife in Many Lands*. 2 volumes. London.

Furnivall, F.J. (1860). 'History of the London Working Men's College' *The Working Men's College Magazine*, 1 November.

Gaffin, J. (1977). 'Women and co-operation' in L. Middleton (ed.) *Women in the Labour Movement*. London, Croom Helm.

Gaffin, J. and Thoms, D. (1983). *Caring and Sharing, The Centenary History of the Co-operative Women's Guild*. Manchester, Co-operative Union.

Gardner, P. (1984). *The Lost Elementary Schools of Victorian England*. Beckenham, Kent, Croom Helm.

Glendinning, V. (1969). *A Suppressed Cry, Life and Death of a Quaker Daughter*. London, Routledge and Kegan Paul.

Goddard, The Rev. C. (1816). *An Account of the Origin, Principles, Proceedings, and Results, of an Institution for Teaching Adults to Read, Established in the Contiguous Parts of Bucks and Berks in 1814*. Windsor, Knight and Son.

Goldstrom, J.M. (1977). 'The content of education and the socialization of the working-class child 1830–1860' in P. McCann (ed.) *Popular Education and Socialization in the Nineteenth Century*. London, Methuen.

Gomersal, M. (1988). 'Ideals and realities: the education of working-class girls, 1800–1870' *History of Education*, Vol. 17, No. 1.

Gorham, D. (1982). *The Victorian Girl and the Feminine Ideal*. London, Croom Helm.

Gorham, D. (1987). 'The ideology of femininity and reading for girls, 1850–1914' in F. Hunt (ed.) *Lessons for Life, The Schooling of Girls and Women 1850–1950*. Oxford, Basil Blackwell.

Gosden, P.H.J.H. (1969). *How They Were Taught*. Oxford, Basil Blackwell.

GPDST (Girls' Public Day School Trust) (n.d.). *Norwich High School 1875–1950*. Norwich, The Goose Press.

GPDST (1972). *The Girls' Public Day School Trust 1872–1972*. London, GPDST.

Grant, J.M., McCutcheon, K.H., Sanders, E.F. (eds) (1927). *St Leonards School 1877–1927*. London, Oxford University Press.

Green, F. (1900). 'Memorabilia' in E.M. Hill (ed.) with the Co-operation of S. Bryant. *Frances Mary Buss Schools' Jubilee Record*. London, Swan Sonnenschein & Co.

Greg, W. (1862). 'Why are women redundant?' reprinted in W.R. Greg, (1868). *Literary and Social Judgments*. London, Trubner and Co.

Grey, Mrs William (Maria) (1871). *On The Education of Women, A Paper Read at the Meeting of the Society of Arts, May 31st 1871*. London, William Ridgway.

Grey, Mrs W. (1874). *Idols of Society; or, Gentility and Femininity*. London, William Ridgway.

Griffin, T. (ed.) *Social Trends 20, 1990 Edition*. London, HMSO.

Grylls, R.G. (1948). *Queen's College 1848-1948*. London, Routledge & Sons.

Guest, R. and John, A.V. (1989). *Lady Charlotte, A Biography of the Nineteenth Century*. London, Weidenfeld and Nicolson.

Hall, R. (1977). *Marie Stopes, A Biography*. London, Andre Deutsch.

Hamer, L. (1967). *Reminiscences of Rawtenstall*. Unpub. manuscript, Rawtenstall, Libraries and Museum Committee.

Hamilton, M.A. (1936). *Newnham, An Informal Biography*. London, Faber and Faber.

Hannam, J. (1989). *Isabella Ford*. Oxford, Basil Blackwell.

Hansard Society Commission Report (1990). *Women at the Top*. London, Hansard Society for Parliamentary Government.

Harrison, J.E. (1925). *Reminiscences of a Student's Life*. London, The Hogarth Press.

Harrison, J.F.C. (1954). *A History of the Working Men's College 1856-1954*. London, Routledge and Kegan Paul.

Hertz, F. (1859). 'Mechanics' institutes for working women, with special reference to the manufacturing districts of Yorkshire', *Transactions of the National Association for the Promotion of Social Science*.

Hewitt, M. 1958. *Wives and Mothers in Victorian Industry*. London, Rockliff.

Hill, E.M. (ed.) with the co-operation of S. Bryant (1900). *Frances Mary Buss Schools' Jubilee Record*. London, Swan Sonnenschein & Co.

'History of the Halifax Working Men's College' (1859). Communicated by the Senior Tutor, *The Working Men's College Magazine*, 1 October.

Hobhouse, H. (1892). 'The working of the Technical Instruction Acts in Somerset' in A.H.D. Acland & H. Llewellyn Smith (eds) (1892). *Studies in Secondary Education*. London, Percival and Co.

Hole, J. (1860). *'Light, More Light!' on the Present State of Education amongst the Working Classes of Leeds*. London, Longman, Green, Longman, and Roberts.

Holyoake, G.J. (n.d. B.L. stamp 1867). *The History of Co-operation in Halifax: and of some other Institutions around it*. London, London Book Store.

Honey, J.R. de S. (1977). *Tom Brown's Universe, The Development of the Public School in the 19th Century*. London, Millington Books.

Horn, P. (1974). *The Victorian Country Child*. Kineton, The Roundwood Press.

Horn, P. (1975). *The Rise and Fall of the Victorian Servant*. Dublin, Gill and Macmillan.

Horn, P. 1978. *Education in Rural England 1800-1914*. New York, St Martin's Press.

Horn, P. (1987). 'Learning their place' *The Times Educational Supplement*, 30 January.

Horn, P. (1988). 'The education and employment of working-class girls, 1870-1914' *History of Education*, Vol. 17, No. 1.

Howarth, J. and Curthoys, M. (1987). 'Gender, curriculum and career: a case study of women university students in England before 1914' in P. Summerfield (ed.) *Women, Education and the Professions*. Leicester, History of Education Society Occasional Publication No. 8.

Howell, M.E. (1957). *Portsmouth High School 1882-1957*. Portsmouth, Grosvenor Press.

Hudson, D. (1972). *Munby, Man of Two Worlds, The Life and Diaries of Arthur J. Munby 1828-1910*. London, John Murray.

Hudson, J.W. (1851). *The History of Adult Education*. London, Longman, Brown, Green and Longmans.

Hughes, M.V. (1978) (first pub. 1946). *A London Girl of the 1880s*. Oxford, Oxford University Press.

Hunt, F. (ed.) (1987). *Lessons for Life, The Schooling of Girls and Women 1850-1950*. Oxford, Basil Blackwell.

Hunt, F. (1987). 'Divided aims: the educational implications of opposing ideologies in girls' secondary schooling' in F. Hunt (ed.) *Lessons for Life, The Schooling of Girls and Women 1850-1950*. Oxford, Basil Blackwell.

Humphries, S. (1981). *Hooligans or Rebels? An Oral History of Working-Class Childhood and Youth 1889-1939*. Oxford, Basil Blackwell.

Hurt, J.S. (1979). *Elementary Schooling and the Working Classes 1860-1918*. London, Routledge and Kegan Paul.

Hyde, Mrs (1862). *How to Win Our Workers: A Short Account of the Leeds Sewing School for Factory Girls*. London, Macmillan and Co.

Jackson, A.H. (1932). *A Victorian Childhood*. London, Methuen and Co.

James, M.E. (1914). *Alice Ottley, First Headmistress of the Worcester High School for Girls, 1883-1912*. London, Longmans.

Jenkins, I. (1953). *The History of the Women's Institute Movement of England and Wales*. Oxford, Oxford University Press.

Jepson, N.A. (1973). *The Beginnings of English University Adult Education, Policy and Problems*. London, Michael Joseph.

Journal of the Women's Education Union, 15 June 1877.

Kamm, J. (1958). *How Different From Us, A Biography of Miss Buss and Miss Beale*. London, The Bodley Head.

Kamm, J. (1971). *Indicative Past, A Hundred Years of the Girls' Public Day School Trust*. London, George Allen & Unwin.

Kean, H. (1990). *Deeds Not Words: the lives of suffragette teachers*. London, Pluto Press.

Kean, H. and Oram, A. (1990). ' "Men must be educated and women must do it": the National Federation (later Union) of Women Teachers and contemporary feminism 1910–30' *Gender and Education*, Vol. 2, No. 2.

Kelly, T. (1957). *George Birkbeck, Pioneer of Adult Education*. Liverpool, Liverpool University Press.

Kelly, T. (1962). *A History of Adult Education in Great Britain*. Liverpool, Liverpool University Press.

Lang, E. (1901). 'The beginnings of the Women's Department' in *The Owens College Jubilee, Being a Special Issue of the Owens College Union Magazine to commemorate the recently accomplished Jubilee of the College*. Manchester, Sherratt and Hughes.

Laqueur, T.W. (1976). *Religion and Respectability, Sunday Schools and Working Class Culture 1780–1850*. New Haven and London, Yale University Press.

Lawson, J. and Silver, H. (1973). *A Social History of Education in England*. London, Methuen.

Layton, Mrs (1931). 'Memories of seventy years' in M. Llewelyn Davies (ed.) *Life as We Have Known It by Co-operative Working Women*. London, Hogarth Press.

Lees, S. and Scott, M. (1990). 'Equal opportunities: rhetoric or action' *Gender and Education*, Vol. 2, No. 3 1990, *Special Issue: Equal Opportunities in Practice* edited by S. Lees and J. Williams.

Leinster-Mackay, D. (1976). 'Dame schools: a need for review' *British Journal of Educational Studies*, Vol. XXIV, No. 1, February.

Levine, P. (1987). *Victorian Feminism 1850–1900*. London, Hutchinson.

Lewis, J. (1980). *The Politics of Motherhood, Child and Maternal Welfare in England, 1900–1939*. London, Croom Helm.

(Lewis, S.) (1840) (8th edn., first pub. 1839). *Woman's Mission*. London, John W. Parker.

Liddington, J. (1984). *The Life and Times of a Respectable Rebel, Selina Cooper 1864–1946*. London, Virago.

Lloyd, E.M. (1928). *Anna Lloyd 1837–1925: A Memoir*. London, Cayne Press.

London Feminist History Group, (1983). *The Sexual Dynamics of History, Men's Power, Women's Resistance*. London, Pluto Press.

Longmans' Domestic Economy Readers for Standards VI and VII (1896). London, Longmans.

Lown, J. (1990). *Women and Industrialization, Gender at Work in Nineteenth-Century England*. Oxford, Polity Press.

Lumsden, L.I. (1927). 'St. Andrews School for Girls' in J.M. Grant, K.H.

McCutcheon and E.F. Sanders (eds) *St Leonards School 1877–1927*. London, Oxford University Press.

Lumsden, L.I. (1933). *Yellow Leaves, Memories of a Long Life*. Edinburgh and London, William Blackwood.

Malim, M.C. and Escreet, H.C. (eds) (1927). *The Book of the Blackheath High School*. London, The Blackheath Press.

Malleson, E. (1926). *Elizabeth Malleson 1828–1916: Autobiographical Notes and Letters, with a Memoir by Hope Malleson*. Printed for private circulation.

Manchester Mechanics' Institution (1846). *Twenty-Second Annual Report of the Directors of the Manchester Mechanics' Institution*. Manchester, Cave and Sever.

Manchester Mechanics' Institution (1863). *Thirty-Ninth Annual Report of the Directors of the Manchester Mechanics' Institution*. Manchester, A. Ireland and Co.

Manchester Mechanics' Institution (1868). *Forty-Fourth Annual Report of the Directors of the Manchester Mechanics' Institution*. Manchester. A. Ireland and Co.

Manchester Mechanics' Institution (1882). *The Fifty-Eighth Annual Report of the Directors of the Manchester Mechanics' Institution*. Manchester, A. Ireland and Co.

Manthorpe, C. (1986). 'Science or domestic science? The struggle to define an appropriate science education for girls in early twentieth-century England' *History of Education*, Vol. 15, No. 3.

Manton, J. (1965). *Elizabeth Garrett Anderson*. London, Methuen and Co.

Marshall, M. Paley (1947). *What I Remember*. Cambridge, Cambridge University Press.

Marshall, S. (ed.) (1980) (first pub. 1967). *Fenland Chronicle, Recollections of William Henry and Kate Mary Edwards Collected and edited by their daughter*. Cambridge, Cambridge University Press.

Martin, F. (1879). 'A college for working women' *Macmillans Magazine*, Part 40.

Martindale, H. (1944). *From One Generation to Another 1839–1944*. London, George Allen and Unwin.

Marx, K. (n.d. first pub. 1848). *Manifesto of the Communist Party*. Moscow, Foreign Languages Publishing House.

Mayhew, H. (1852). 'Home is home, be it never so homely' in Viscount Ingestre (ed.) *Meliora; or Better Times to Come. Being the Contributions of Many Men Touching the Present State and Prospects of Society*. London, John Parker and Son.

Maynard, C.L. (1910). *Between College Terms*. London, James Nisbet and Co.

McCrone, K.E. (1988). *Sport and the Physical Emancipation of English Women 1870–1914*. London, Routledge.

Mechanics' Magazine, letter to the editor, 12 June 1830.

Merson, E. (1979). *Once There Was . . . the Village School*. Southampton, Paul Cave Publications.

Milburn, J. (1969). 'The Secondary Schoolmistress: a study of her Professional Views and their Significance in the Educational Developments of the Period'. Unpub. Ph.D. Thesis, University of London.

Miles, S. and Middleton, C. (1990). 'Girls' education in the balance: The ERA and inequality' in M. Flude and M. Hammer (eds) *The Education Reform Act 1988, Its Origins and Implications*. Lewes, Falmer Press.

Moore, Dr W. (1886). 'Address to the British Medical Association, Fifty-Fourth Annual Meeting, Brighton 1886' *The Lancet*, 14 August.

Mort, F. (1987). *Dangerous Sexualities, Medico-Moral Politics in England Since 1830*. London, Routledge & Kegan Paul.

A Mother (1868). 'Defects in the moral training of girls', in Rev. Shipley, (ed.) *The Church and the World*. London, Longmans, Green, Reader and Dyer.

Muir, Prof. J. (1950). *John Anderson: Pioneer of Technical Education and the College he Founded*, edited by J.M. Macaulay. Glasgow, John Smith and Son.

Murray, M. (1963). *My First Hundred Years*. London, William Kimber.

Nash, R. (1907). 'Co-operator and citizen' in B. Villiers (ed.) *The Case for Women's Suffrage*. London, T. Fisher Unwin.

National Association for the Promotion of Social Science (1880). *Transactions of the Manchester Meeting, 1879*. London, Longmans, Green and Co.

National Society for Promoting the Education of the Poor in the Principles of the Established Church (1812). *First Annual Report of the National Society for Promoting the Education of the Poor in the Principles of the Established Church*. London, The Free School.

National Society for Promoting the Education of the Poor in the Principles of the Established Church (1814). *Second Annual Report (1813)*. London, The Free School.

Oakley, A. (1976) (first pub. 1974). *Housewife*. Harmondsworth, Penguin Books.

Okely, J. (1983) (first pub. 1979). 'Privileged, schooled and finished: boarding education for girls' in J. Purvis and M. Hales (eds) *Achievement and Inequality in Education*. London, Routledge and Kegan Paul.

Owen, P. (1988). ' "Who would be free, herself must strike the blow": the National Union of Women Teachers, equal pay, and women within the teaching profession' *History of Education*, Vol. 17, No. 1, March.

PP (Parliamentary Papers) 1845 XXXV.

PP 1861 XXI, I.

PP (1864). *Reports of the Inspectors of Factories for the Half Term Ending 31st October 1863*. Vol. XXII.

(Parkes, B. Rayner) (1854). *Remarks on the Education of Girls*. London, John Chapman.

Peck, W. (1952). *A Little Learning or A Victorian Childhood*. London, Faber and Faber.

Pedersen, J.S. (1987). *The Reform of Girls' Secondary and Higher Education in Victorian England, A Study of Elites and Educational Change*. New York and London, Garland Publishing, Series of Outstanding Dissertations.

Peel, Mrs C.S. (1933). *Life's Enchanted Cup, An Autobiography (1872–1933)*. London, John Lane, The Bodley Head.

Penn, M. (1979). Facsimile edition of the original pub. in 1947. *Manchester Fourteen Miles*. Firle, Sussex, Caliban Books.

Percival, A.C. (1939). *The English Miss To-Day and Yesterday. Ideals, Methods, and Personalities in the Education and Upbringing of Girls during the Last Hundred Years*. London, George Harrap and Co.

Percy, K. (1970). 'The prehistory of the evening institute' *Studies in Adult Education*, Vol. 2, No. 2.

Peterson, M.J. (1973). 'The Victorian governess: status incongruence in family and society' in M. Vicinus (ed.) (first pub. 1972). *Suffer and Be Still, Women in the Victorian Age*. Bloomington and London, Indiana University Press.

Phillips, A. (ed.) (1979). *A Newnham Anthology*. Cambridge, Cambridge University Press.

Pinchbeck, I. (1930). *Women Workers and the Industrial Revolution 1750–1850*. London, Routledge and Sons.

Pole, T. (1813). *An Address to the Committee of the Bristol Society for Teaching the Adult Poor to Read the Holy Scriptures*. Bristol, C. McDowall.

Pole, T. (1816) (sec. ed.). *A History of the Origin and Progress of Adult Schools*. Bristol, C. McDowall.

Porter, W.S. (1922). *Sheffield Literary and Philosophical Society: A Centenary Retrospect 1822–1922*. Sheffield, Northend.

Purvis, J. (1980). 'Working-class women and adult education in nineteenth-century Britain' *History of Education*, Vol. 9, No. 3.

Purvis, J. (1981). ' "Women's life is essentially domestic, public life being confined to men" (Comte): separate spheres and inequality in the education of working-class women, 1854–1900' *History of Education*, Vol. 10, No. 4.

Purvis, J. (1981a). 'Towards a history of women's education in nineteenth-century Britain: a sociological analysis' *Westminister Studies in Education*, Vol. 4, 1981.

Purvis, J. (1981b). 'The double burden of class and gender in the schooling of working-class girls in nineteenth-century England, 1800–1870' in L. Barton and S. Walker (eds) *Schools, Teachers and Teaching*. Lewes, Falmer Press.

Purvis, J. (1981c). 'Women and teaching in the nineteenth century' in R. Dale, C. Esland, R. Fergusson and M. MacDonald (eds) (1981). *Education and the State, Volume 2, Politics, Patriarchy and Practice*. Lewes, Falmer Press.

Purvis, J. (1984). 'The experience of schooling for working-class boys and girls in nineteenth-century England' in I.F. Goodson and S.J. Ball (eds) *Defining the Curriculum, Histories and Ethnographies*. Lewes, Falmer Press.

Purvis, J. (1985). 'Domestic subjects since 1870' in I.F. Goodson (ed.) *Social Histories of the Secondary Curriculum, Subjects for Study*. Lewes, Falmer Press.

Purvis, J. (1989). *Hard Lessons, The Lives and Education of Working-Class Women in Nineteenth-Century England*. Oxford, Polity Press.

Raikes, E. (1908). *Dorothea Beale of Cheltenham*. London, Archibald Constable and Co.

Ramsey, G.M.N. (1927). 'Foundation and government' in J.M. Grant, K.H. McCutcheon and E.F. Sanders (eds) *St Leonards School 1877–1927*. London, Oxford University Press.

Rankin, M.C. (n.d., c. 1900). *The Art and Practice of Laundry Work*. London, Blackie and Son.

(Ranyard, Mrs) L.N.R. (1859). *The Missing Link; Or, Bible-Women in the Homes of the London Poor*. London, James Nisbet and Co.

Raverat, G. (1960). *Period Piece, A Cambridge Childhood*. London, Faber and Faber.

Rendall, J. (1985). *The Origins of Modern Feminism: Women in Britain, France and the United States, 1780–1860*. London, Macmillan.

Reynolds, K.M. (1950). 'The school and its place in girls' education' in R.M. Scrimgeour (ed.) *The North London Collegiate School 1850–1950, A Hundred Years of Girls' Education*. London, Oxford University Press.

Roberts, R.D. (1891). *Eighteen Years of University Extension*. Cambridge, Cambridge University Press.

Roberts, E. (1984). *A Woman's Place: An Oral History of Working-Class Women 1890–1940*. Oxford, Basil Blackwell.

Rogers, A.M.A.H. (1938). *Degrees by Degrees*. Oxford, Oxford University Press.

Rossiter, E. (1859). 'A student's wife's notion of college and classes' *The Working Men's College Magazine*, 1 October.

Rowbotham, S. (1981). 'Travellers in a strange country: working-class students, 1873–1910' *History Workshop Journal*, 12, Autumn.

Rowbotham, T. (1859). 'Account of the origin and progress of the People's College at Sheffield' *The Working Men's College Magazine*, April.

Rowntree, J.W. and Binns, H.B. (1903). *A History of the Adult School Movement*. London, Headley Brothers.

Royal Commission on Secondary Education (Bryce Commission). *PP 1895* Vol. XLVIII.

Ruskin, J. (1865). *Sesame and Lilies*. London, Smith, Elder and Co.

Russell, B. and P. (1937). *The Amberley Papers: Bertrand Russell's Family Background Vol. 2*. London, Allen and Unwin.

Sadler, M. (ed.) (1908, sec. ed.). *Continuation Schools in England and Elsewhere, Their Place in the Educational System of an Industrial and Commercial State*. Manchester, Manchester University Press.

Sanderson, M. (1972). *The Universities and British Industry 1850–1970*. London, Routledge and Kegan Paul.

Schools Inquiry Commission Report, *PP 1867–68*.

Sewell, E.M. (1865). *Principles of Education, Drawn from Nature and Revelation, and Applied to Female Education in the Upper Classes*. 2 Vols. London, Longmans, Green, Longman, Roberts and Green.

Sewell, S. (1868). *Women and the Times We Live In*, extract reprinted in J. Horowitz Murray (ed.) (1984, first pub. 1982). *Strong-Minded Women and Other Lost Voices from 19th-Century England*. Harmondsworth, Penguin Books.

Sharp, E. (1926). *Hertha Ayrton 1854–1923*. London, Edward Arnold and Co.

Shaw, C. (1977) (first pub. 1903). *When I was a Child*. Firle, Sussex, Caliban Books.

Shepherd, R.H. (ed.) (1870). *Speeches Literary and Social by Charles Dickens*. London, John Camden Hotten.

Shillito, M.E. (1950). 'The Frances Mary Buss House' in R.M. Scrimgeour (ed.) (1950). *The North London Collegiate School 1850–1950*. London, Oxford University Press.

Sidgwick, Mrs H. (1901). 'The higher education of women' in R.D. Roberts (ed.) *Education in the Nineteenth Century*. Cambridge, Cambridge University Press.

Sillitoe, H. (1933). *A History of the Teaching of Domestic Subjects*. London, Methuen.

Smiles, S. (1859). *Self-Help; with Illustrations of Character and Conduct*. London, John Murray.

Smiles, S. (1871). *Character*. London, John Murray.

S.S. (Smiles, S.) (1843). 'The women of the working classes' *The Union*, Vol. 1, No. 10, 1 January.

Smith, M. (1892). *The Autobiography of Mary Smith, Schoolmistress and Nonconformist*. Carlisle, Wordsworth Press.

Sokoloff, B. (1987). *Edith and Stepney, The Life of Edith Ramsey*. London, Stepney Books.

St John-Brooks, C. (1988). 'Cry freedom for changes in boarding school life' *The Sunday Times*, 29 May.

Stack, V.E. (ed.) (1963). *Oxford High School, GPDST, 1875–1960*. Oxford, printed privately.

Stanworth, M. (1984). 'Women and class analysis: a reply to John Goldthorpe' *Sociology*, Vol. 18, No. 2.

Steadman, F. Cecily (1931). *In The Days of Miss Beale, A Study of her Work and Influence*. London, E.J. Burrow and Co.

Steer, F.W. (1962). *The Chichester Literary and Philosophical Society and Mechanics' Institute*. Chichester, Chichester City Council.

Stephen, B. (1927). *Emily Davies and Girton College*. London, Constable and Co.

Stott, M. (1978). *Organization Woman, The Story of the National Union of Townswomen's Guilds*. London, Heinemann.

Strachey, R. (1928). *'The Cause', A Short History of the Women's Movement in Great Britain*. London, G. Bell & Sons.

Strachey, R. (1931). *Millicent Garrett Fawcett*. London, John Murray.

Stuart, J. (1911). *Reminiscences*. London, printed for private circulation at the Chiswick Press.

Sturt, M. (1967). *The Education of the People: A History of Primary Education in England and Wales in the Nineteenth Century*. London, Routledge and Kegan Paul.

Supplement to The Working Men's College Magazine, 1 April 1859.

Sutherland, G. (1971). *Elementary Education in the Nineteenth Century*. London, The Historical Association.

Sutherland, G. (1987). 'The movement for the higher education of women: its social and intellectual context in England, c. 1840–80' in P.J. Waller (ed.) *Politics and Social Change in Modern Britain*. Brighton, Harvester Press.

Syrett, N. (1939). *The Sheltering Tree*. London, Geoffrey Bles.

Taking Liberties Collective (1989). *Learning the Hard Way, Women's Oppression in Men's Education*. London, Macmillan.

Taylor, K. (1982). 'Memoir' in J. Burnett (ed.) *Destiny Obscure, Autobiographies of Childhood, Education and Family from the 1820s to the 1920s*. London, Allen Lane.

The Good Sunday Scholars (n.d.). London, Religious Tract Society.

'The new school for wives'. (1852). *Household Words*, March.

Theobald, M.R. (1988). 'The accomplished woman and the propriety of intellect: a new look at women's education in Britain and Australia, 1800–1850' *History of Education*, Vol. 17, No. 1, March.

'The profession of an English matron' (1871). *The Saturday Review*, 20 May.

Thompson, E.P. (1972) (first pub. 1963). *The Making of the English Working Class*. Harmondsworth, Pelican Books.

Thompson, F. (1954) (first pub. 1945). *Lark Rise to Candleford*. London, Oxford University Press.

Thompson, J. (1983). *Learning Liberation, Women's Response to Men's Education*. London, Croom Helm.

Thompson, T. (ed.) (1987). *Dear Girl, The Diaries and Letters of Two Working Women 1897–1917*. London, The Women's Press.

Tomlinson, S. (1983). 'Black women in higher education – case studies of university women in Britain' in L. Barton and S. Walker (eds) *Race, Class and Education*. London, Croom Helm.

Toplis, G. (ed.) (1896). *Leaves from the Notebooks of Frances M. Buss*. London, Macmillan and Co.

'Treatment of women', *Eliza Cook's Journal*, 9 August 1851.

Tuke, M.J. (1939). *A History of Bedford College for Women 1849–1937*. London, Oxford University Press.

Turnbull, A. (1980). 'Home economics – training for womanhood?' in C. Love, D. Smith and A. Turnbull (eds) *Women in the Making*, South Bank Sociology Occasional Paper 2. London, Social Sciences Department, Polytechnic of the South Bank.

Turnbull, A. (1987). 'Learning her womanly work: the elementary school curriculum, 1870–1914' in F. Hunt (ed.) *Lessons for Life, The Schooling of Girls and Women 1850–1950*. Oxford, Basil Blackwell.

Turner, B. (1974). *Equality for Some: The Story of Girls' Education*. London, Ward Lock Educational.

Tylecote, M. (1957). *The Mechanics' Institutes of Lancashire and Yorkshire Before 1851*. Manchester, Manchester University Press.

Universities Central Council on Admissions (UCCA) (1989). *Statistical Supplement to the Twenty-Sixth Report 1987–8*. Cheltenham, UCCA.

Vicinus, M. (1985). *Independent Women, Work and Community for Single Women, 1850–1920*. London, Virago.

Walby, S. (1986). 'Gender, class and stratification' in R. Crompton and M. Mann (eds) *Gender and Stratification*. Oxford, Polity Press.

Wallington, E. (1874). 'The physical and intellectual capacities of woman equal to those of man' *Anthropologia*, 1.

Walvin, J. (1978). *A Child's World: A Social History of English Childhood 1800–1914*. Harmondsworth, Penguin Books.

Warnock, Mrs H.M. (1972). 'Oxford' in The Girls' Public Day School Trust. *The Girls' Public Day School Trust*. London, GPDST.

Watts, R. (1980). 'The Unitarian contribution to the development of female education, 1790–1850' *History of Education*, Vol. 9, No. 4.

Watts, R. (1989). 'Knowledge is power – Unitarians, gender and education in the eighteenth and early nineteenth centuries' *Gender and Education*, Vol. 1, No. 1.

Webb, C. (1927). *The Woman with the Basket, The History of the Women's Co-operative Guild 1883–1927*. Manchester, Co-operative Wholesale Society.

Weeks, J. (1981). *Sex, Politics and Society*. Harlow, Essex, Longman.

Weiner, G. (1989). 'Feminism, equal opportunities and vocationalism: the changing context' in H. Burchell and V. Millman (eds) *Changing Perspectives on Gender, New Initiatives in Secondary Education*. Milton Keynes, Open University Press.

Westaway, K.M. (1932). *A History of Bedford High School*. Bedford, F.R. Hockliffe.

Whibley, C. (1894). 'The farce of university extension: a rejoinder' *Nineteenth Century*. Vol. 36, July–December.

Widdowson, F. (1980). *Going Up Into the Next Class: Women and Elementary Teacher Training 1840-1914*. London, Women's Resource and Resources Centre Publications.

Wilkinson, E. (1938). 'Ellen Wilkinson' in The Countess of Oxford and Asquith (ed.) *Myself When Young by Famous Women of To-Day*, London, Frederick Muller.

Williams, P. (1987). 'Pioneer women students at Cambridge, 1869-81' in F. Hunt (ed.) *Lessons for Life, The Schooling of Girls and Women 1850-1950*. Oxford, Basil Blackwell.

Wilson, A. (1981). 'Annie Wilson' in T. Thompson, *Edwardian Childhoods*. London, Routledge & Kegan Paul.

Wilson, E. (1977). *Women and the Welfare State*. London, Tavistock.

Wober, M. (1971). *English Girls' Boarding Schools*. London, Allen Lane, The Penguin Press.

Woodham-Smith, C. (1950). *Florence Nightingale 1820-1910*. London, Constable.

The Working Men's College Journal, December 1900.

Wrigley, Mrs 'A plate-layer's wife' in M. Llewelyn Davies (ed.) (1931). *Life As We Have Known It by Co-operative Working Women*. London, Hogarth Press.

Yorkshire Union of Mechanics' Institutes. (1846, 1847, 1852, 1857, 1858, 1859, 1861, 1862). *Reports*. Leeds, Edward Baines and Sons.

Zimmern, A. (1898). *The Renaissance of Girls' Education in England, A Record of Fifty Years' Progress*. London, A.D. Innes and Co.

Zouche, D.E. de (1955). *Roedean School 1885-1955*. Brighton, The Dolphin Press.

Index